CYBER CHURCH

CHRISTIANITY AND THE INTERNET

Dr Patrick Dixon

KINGSWAY PUBLICATIONS
EASTBOURNE

ISBN 0 85476 711 8

Co-published in South Africa with
SCB Publishers
Cornelis Struik House, 80 McKenzie Street
Cape Town 8001, South Africa.
Reg no 04/02203/06

Designed and produced by Bookprint Creative Services
P.O. Box 827, BN21 3YJ, England for
KINGSWAY PUBLICATIONS LTD
Lottbridge Drove, Eastbourne, East Sussex BN23 6NT.
Printed in Great Britain.

To Sheila,
my best friend, closest advisor
and source of endless encouragement

Acknowledgements

I am deeply grateful to Professor Prabhu Guptara for the discussions at various stages on technology, the Internet and faith that directly gave rise to this book. I would also particularly like to thank Chris Thackery for a number of the ideas contained in this book, for his numerous suggestions at draft stage and for substantial editorial involvement.

Statistics in this book have been derived largely from the Internet itself and from recent publications.

Contents

The Future Is Here

CHAPTER 1

Taking the World by Storm

Cyberchurch:
1. The body of all Christians who interact using global computer networks (cyber, of computer communications; church, body of all Christians)
2. An electronically linked group of believers, aiming to reproduce in cyberspace some aspects of conventional church life.

Internet:
A global network of millions of computer users.

Cyberspace:
The electronic world created by those who use the Internet.

Cyberchurch is here

I sit down at my desk in front of my computer, ready to start work. With a click of the mouse I'm on the Internet: I'm connected to tens of thousands of computers, millions of people all across the globe, and unimaginable resources of information – all for the price of a local phone call.

Someone who has just joined my church has an autistic son. I type in 'Autism' as a search word and within seconds I'm reading information about what autism is, and simultaneously printing out a list of help groups for parents, and details of the latest research in America. I'm ready to brief the church.

I have a friend on the mission field in a remote part of Africa who wants information about malaria drugs. I send him an e-mail with the details, and some family news. There's no need to wait weeks for a letter to arrive; no need to try and catch him when he's near a phone; no need to worry about time zones. The message is there in minutes, waiting for him to read it when he's ready.

I decide to work on my sermon, and with a few clicks of my mouse I have access to online Bibles and concordances, even the Dead Sea Scrolls. Maybe I can glean some inspiration from the sermons of Wesley, all here on the Internet.

I've arranged a conference with some church leaders. I connect up and we talk. I can see their faces on my screen, and thanks to the small camera mounted on my computer, they can see me.

I check my own e-mail box, where I find several messages from people who have seen my Internet pages. I type my e-mail replies.

Someone in my church is looking for work as a graphic designer. I search the Internet and track down a dozen likely looking companies in minutes. And in a few moments I have forwarded his CV to all of them simultaneously.

I connect through to a cyberchurch service in Canada. I'm greeted by a photograph of the congregation and a list of options. Through the speakers attached to my computer I hear background music sent direct from the church. A few seconds later I'm following the lines of a song on the screen, and listening to congregational singing. After that I settle down to listen to a talk, with lecture notes to follow on my screen. I can leave a prayer request if I want to.

I decide to take a short break. I click with the mouse again and I'm connected to a video camera in San Francisco. I relax while I watch the sun rise over the Bay, gilding the Golden Gate bridge . . . .

The future is already here. And this glimpse of cyberchurch is just the tip of an iceberg of incredible proportions. The Internet revolution is taking the world by storm, and is creating new products, new lifestyles, new ways of meeting people, new perspectives on 'reality'. The Internet is the greatest new market ever to emerge in the history of humankind. It is growing faster than anyone can measure, in ways beyond the comprehension of any previous generation.

For years people have talked of the information age, but they have usually meant a world where there are computers in every home and televisions in every living room. What is happening is on a vastly different scale. Today the prospect is in sight of complete access to unbelievable knowledge, at any time, at any place in the world or in outer space – for free. Everything that collects information is being connected electronically to everything that delivers it. This is already producing some bizarre results.

Traffic cameras on my screen

I can look at traffic cameras on my screen at home before making a journey across a city. I can check whether the sun is shining on a beach the other side of the world. I can see with my own eyes whether a colleague is sitting at his desk in another nation before I talk to him. I can watch the needle flicker on a seismograph in San Francisco. I can examine the surface of the original Dead Sea Scrolls in Israel. I can read the official government inspector's report on my children's school. I can watch an action replay of some of the Atlanta Olympics' greatest moments, or read the latest scientific research on human cloning experiments.

Soon I may also be able to see a spy satellite picture taken directly above my own home, showing me the activities of my neighbours, how many vehicles are parked in a nearby street, the progress of a building project and the state of harvesting on a friend's farm. Admittedly there is likely to be a charge for such premium pictures, but the current rate of £2,500 a picture is likely to fall dramatically when the satellite computers are wired to the Internet.

Where is it all going?

We need to look deeply at what is already happening, to examine this new electronic world. In time, it will affect most aspects of the way we live and probably even change the way we think. Our world is being transformed. Whatever our personal views, we need to understand and to make an informed Christian response.

What are the opportunities for the church that this revolution is creating? What is the potential for evangelism on the Internet? How will these changes affect our communications and the way we work as Christians? And what about cyberaddiction and online pornography? Are we heading for a world of virtual reality church, where no one ever meets except on a computer screen linked by telephone; where there is an unbridgeable gap between the world of cyberchurch and the world of normal life, a kind of pseudo-Christian existence which denies the very basis of local Christian community? Such things are already within the grasp of new technology. A recent survey by Motorola indicated that about three-quarters of the population are uncomfortable about the Internet in some way. Are these fears grounded?

This book aims to explore these questions. But first we need to have an understanding of what the Internet is and how it is transforming the world in which we live. Chapters 2 and 3 examine the technology already in place and that which is fast approaching, and look at its impact. Chapters 4–7 look at the enormous possibilities for the church generated by this change. Chapters 8–12 address the very real fears and concerns that people have about where all this is leading.

The Motorola survey also indicated that many people feel they ought to know more about the Internet than they do. My hope is that this book will go some way towards helping people who feel like that.

CHAPTER 2

A Tour of Cyberworld

As one people speaking the same language . . . nothing they plan to do will be impossible (Genesis 11:6).

Fighting a massive nuclear war

How did it all begin? The Internet was never intended for the kind of use it has today. It was developed by the Pentagon over thirty years ago at the height of the Cold War as a major defensive weapon. The idea was to protect the US military from a massive nuclear strike which could wipe out many major cities, not just in the US but in other nations. Nuclear weapons were known to produce huge electromagnetic pulses which could possibly disable or destroy complex electrical equipment large distances away from the explosion and from areas of obvious destruction. Computer experts were asked to devise a defence system which could operate, however many communication centres were destroyed, compromised or taken over by the enemy.

Global network to beat the bomb

The result was ingenious. They dreamed up a vast network where it was impossible to predict the direction in which information would travel. Data would be switched in milliseconds from one section of route to another, and every message would be sent as hundreds or thousands of tiny packets. These could be scattered across many different routes, and then be reassembled in the right order when they all arrived. If some packets were destroyed on the way, then the receiving computer would be alerted to which ones they were. Hopefully, however severe the state of hostilities, enough packets would get through to enable the fight to continue.

As Cold War tensions eased, other public bodies, especially academic institutions such as universities, were given permission to connect their own considerable computer resources to the Internet. This revolutionised the exchange of information for research purposes. Expansion continued, broadening in scope all the time.

Today that network is public, but the design is the same. Instead of a few hundred Pentagon computers there are now at least 25,000 publicly available Internet host computers. Instead of them all being commanded by one government, they are owned by thousands of different companies in different nations, with no common agreement on standards or content – except that all the design features of the original system should be preserved. Indeed, the Internet investment is now so vast and so global that it would be extremely difficult to change the Internet infrastructure. Instead, companies like Netscape have been adding hundreds of new features such as sound and graphics capabilities.

The global village arrives

The global village has finally arrived – in cyberspace. The Internet has shrunk the world dramatically. When my computer is connected I have no idea where the next piece of information is going to come from. It might be from information already sitting there in the computer disk drive on my desk, or it might be from a university computer not far from my home. However, it is just as likely to be coming via satellite and fibre optic links from Sydney, New York, Kansas City, Paris, Moscow or Hong Kong.

In the course of ten or fifteen minutes it is not uncommon for me to be connected to computers in ten or more nations. It all costs the same – almost nothing – however long the link. The speed is almost identical, whether the link is 300 or 3,000 miles away.

Using the Internet, I can send e-mail (electronic mail) anywhere around the world in a few minutes. I can subscribe to newsgroups. These are Internet discussion forums on every imaginable subject from philosophy to flying saucers. I can discuss, argue and debate whatever subject I choose, with people all over the world whom I have never met or whose voice I have never heard. Using Telnet software, I can log on from my own home to a computer in Wyoming or Hong Kong and use it as if I were there at a terminal in person. And using File Transfer Protocol (FTP) software I can send computer files in a standard format across the globe. Using Internet Relay Chat (IRC) I can have a live link to someone across the other side of the world, communicating by typing messages on our keyboards.

Probably the best-known component of the Internet is the World Wide Web, a massive market-place of information, services, advertising, ideas, news and entertainment from anywhere in the world. All this is accessed by a few clicks of a computer mouse, using browser software such as *Netscape* or *Microsoft Explorer*.

And what we are seeing now is just the very beginning.

A moral responsibility

We need to face up to this. We cannot ignore the Internet, no matter how uncomfortable it may make us feel personally. This technology is already coming to dominate the lives of some people in our churches and in communities we are seeking to reach. We have a moral obligation to understand this global revolution and to make a Christian response. Without this response, we risk becoming increasingly marginalised and being seen as irrelevant by the people we are seeking to reach.

So, then, what can technology do today and how will it alter tomorrow? We need to have a grasp of this to have any hope of finding answers to the 'spiritual' issues regarding use and abuse of the technology. We need more than just a snapshot view of what is available today. It is vital for us to catch a sense of momentum, of direction; a feel for the shape of the future. The rest of this chapter aims to do just that.

From 1978 to 1998 to ?

Sometimes it is helpful to look back a few years in order to see more clearly the accelerating pace of technological progress. In 1978 I was working with one of the world's first microcomputers. It had 32,000 characters of memory (bytes) on a large board of microchips, and a further 250,000 on a pair of floppy disks. The computer on my desk now has 16 million bytes of memory on chips and 1,600 million more in a sealed disk unit. It cost a fraction of the original 1978 model. In January 1996 the price of a single chip holding 4 million bytes (equivalent to four volumes of *Encyclopaedia Britannica*) fell from $43 to just $13, and is now even less.

Computer power doubles every eighteen months

Over the last twenty years computer power has doubled every eighteen months. If that rate continues, then in twenty years' time it will be possible to buy a box half the size of a mobile phone, which is able to contain the entire contents of every book, magazine and newspaper ever written in the entire history of the world – and all for less than the cost of a desk-top computer today. The information revolution will have fully dawned.

People may say that we will have no use for it all, but that merely indicates a lack of imagination: after all, who hasn't at some time or another been frustrated by a lack of information? Networking information on this scale would open up undreamed of possibilities.

Faster Internet connections

Connections to the Internet, and between computers on the system, are all gaining rapidly in speed. But traffic is increasing even faster, so actual performance is falling, particularly at certain times of the day. Every few weeks another huge highway is opened, and within days the traffic on it is so great that traffic jams are beginning to form. These are all healthy signs of growth, not terminal signs of collapse. In August 1996 there was a scare when a major US Internet provider crashed for over twelve hours. But such things have always been an accepted way of life with emerging technologies.

Here are some speed comparisons:

1988 modem	2,200 bits per second
1994 modem	14,400 bits per second
1996 modem	28,800 bits per second (commonest on sale today)
1996 ISDN	128,000 bits per second
1996 cable modems	30 million bits per second
1996 ATM	155 million bits per second

One thing is certain: whether you have your own connection or not, the Internet will soon follow you wherever you go. If you fly in a plane you are likely to find the Net staring at you on a flat screen attached to the seat in front. If you book a hotel room, it is likely to be as much a standard part of the package as satellite TV or a movie channel.

Removing the bottlenecks

Up until now the amount of data that can be sent down copper wires in a conventional phone system has been a major bottleneck, but this is set to change. Fibre optic cable, laid by cable TV companies, is now available to millions of homes, just waiting to be exploited. Cable power is wasted on mere one-way television watching when it promises so much more.

For those without cable, ISDN technology allows data speeds up to five times faster than the fastest modem using phone wires. However, even ISDN is being rapidly overtaken. There are already devices on the market allowing data transfer a thousand times faster than the modem I use on my own computer today. British Telecom have recently announced new technology which will allow the standard telephone line to handle as much data as the fibre optic cables laid by cable TV companies. It will cost £400 to buy and install the receiver equipment for your home, and will be available in less than two years. With these developments, the Internet will one day be delivering high-resolution, wide-screen, interactive television channels as well as all the other services.

20 million copies down the phone

It is hard to grasp the sheer scale of Internet activity. Computers process information by breaking it down into small packages called 'bits'. The Internet already handles 15 million, million, million bits per day. Another illustration, indeed one of the most spectacular online software distributions in computer history, happened between 1994 and 1996 when more than 20 million people downloaded a program called *Navigator*, a viewing system provided by a company called Netscape for users of the World Wide Web. Of course, even the fastest computer in the world would have had difficulty coping with that amount of traffic, especially as each copy took up to an hour on the phone to send and receive.

The problem was not just computer power, but the number of lines which the computer could handle at once, plus the limited capacity of the telephone network itself. The solution was simple: let people take their own copies onto other large computers in different countries, and let them become distributors themselves.

Microsoft hit back with the latest version of its own browser called *Explorer*. In the month of July 1996 so many people downloaded *Explorer* that Netscape Navigator's market share fell from 78% to 73%, while *Explorer*'s share rose from 8% to 16%.

This kind of distribution is a life-saver to software manufacturers because programs can now sometimes go out of date in fewer than six weeks – less time than a product stays on the shelves of a retailer. In many cases recently I have returned home after buying a program, only to discover that I cannot use it without downloading vital added features via the Net. The rapid growth in the speed and power of the Internet will have a huge impact on the production and marketing of software.

Why bother to buy programs in boxes?

The scene is changing so fast that sometimes one begins to wonder if there is any point in loading the software in a box at all. *Dr Solomon's Anti-Virus Toolkit* is a recent case in point. This is designed to detect all the latest computer viruses, which means that the virus files need constantly updating – several times a year.

A week after registering I was sent another set of disks completely replacing the old ones and requiring another installation. They have since sent me two further sets of disks. Online updates are more efficient, but at the time of writing the company obviously feels that not enough people have modems yet to make it their standard way of operating. But in the longer term, buying disks and CD-ROMs in boxes will seem old fashioned and needlessly wasteful of the earth's resources.

Of course, Christian organisations likewise will want to take advantage of the massive savings on costs, time and natural resources by distributing information, software, interactive training materials, etc. via the Internet. We will return to this later.

Programs hidden in pages of text

However, the most exciting development is not download-ing whole programs, but sending tiny programs to do specific tasks. For example, anyone phoning my own web-site (http://people.delphi.com/patrickdixon) sees a caption on a page about genetics: 'Every few minutes another human gene is decoded'.

For added effect I wanted a clock to appear on the screen, so I included an applet in my page of text. This little program is invisible to the user and only takes a couple of seconds to send. Once inside the person's com-puter, it finds out the right time (from the computer clock, different in every time zone), draws the face of a clock and displays the user's local time automatically.

The clock is just a gimmick, but software manufacturers are quaking at the possibilities. In future, perhaps no one will bother buying a vacuum-packed set of disks and manuals from a computer shop, especially as many pro-grams contain hundreds of features that people rarely use or ever learn about. This is system overkill, and just fills up hard disks, as well as slowing programs down.

No more hard disks and manuals?

In future, many people will have a far simpler computer system, which they connect online before selecting what they want to do. They may not need any hard disk or manuals. If they want to use a word-processor, for exam-ple, they may just 'rent' the sections of the program that they need for a tiny sum each day. The program would be downloaded into the machine and would stay there for a limited number of hours or days before terminating. Such a computer system could be as small as a mobile phone with a special pad and screen.

The cost savings on software production, warehousing and distribution will be enormous. Every piece of code used will be that week's latest version, so there will be no more hassles correcting bugs in previously installed systems. Everything you do will then be instantly upgradable. You will always have access to the most sophisticated and powerful software just when you really need it – not any earlier, and not for any longer than you need it either.

Software piracy through illegal disk copying will also be controllable, because all commercial code downloaded will have an automatic self-destruct mechanism within it. This could save software companies billions of dollars a year in distribution costs and lost revenue.

My computer is becoming more intelligent

It is already true that most times I connect to the Net, my computer becomes more intelligent, learning new tricks as I go along. This can open up new possibilities. For example, when I visited a cyberchurch recently, the site required a special piece of computer code to be running on my machine in order for me to hear the worship they were sending me.

My computer had already learned that trick when visiting a music site the previous week, so the sound came out of the speakers automatically. If there had been a problem, the cyberchurch site would have automatically detected that my computer was uncertain what to do next and would have offered to teach it how to listen to the data and turn it into music.

Is Big Brother listening?

Of course it is not only the software business which is being transformed. The rapidly increasing capabilities of the Internet will affect the whole of the commercial world.

The Internet is already big business. By early 1997 around 3 million people were already buying and selling goods on the Net. Just one click with a mouse is all it takes to pay by credit card. In the early days there were huge worries about security, until the invention of mathematical encryption schemes such as *Pretty Good Privacy* by Paul Zimmerman.

This is so powerful that the US government tried to prosecute him for exporting a 'military weapon'. The CIA and FBI were afraid that they would be powerless against crooks and terrorists. They had visions of criminals and foreign armies being able to send coded messages to each other around the world, using US computers and telephone systems, without being able to decipher what they were saying.

The court case collapsed after the US authorities realised that tens of thousands of people had already downloaded the program from dozens of different sites around the world, and were using it on their own computers.

Pretty Good Privacy is a clever system. It works using very large prime numbers and, used at its highest level, is almost impossible to crack in less than several months, and that is only by using a whole battery of computers day and night. Even then, only one message is decoded. Everything else before and after that transmission remains secure.

This obviously raises immense issues for Christians regarding the uses to which the Internet can be put. In later chapters we will look both at censorship of pornography and subversive materials, and also, on the other side of the coin, the Internet's potential for penetrating areas hostile to the gospel.

Buying and selling on the Net

As we have seen, the Internet is already used widely to trade and persuade. The value of the trade in 1996 was around $1 billion, with growth expected to reach anywhere between $7 billion and $170 billion a year by early next century.

Music sales are popular. One site sells 25,000 CDs every day, allowing people to hear samples before they order. The world's busiest site is a CD site, able to send out a staggering 100 megabits every second – that is the equivalent of 6,000 volumes of *Encyclopaedia Britannica* every minute. Magazines are also picking up large readerships. Just a few months after launch, the electronic EMAP magazine collection was receiving 350,000 'hits' or different access requests every week.

Internet advertising

The driving force behind the development of the Internet is, increasingly, advertising. While many Internet sites at the moment are run by companies looking to sell their own products (banks are a good example), others have been set up to sell advertising space just like any other media company. An example might be a virtual reality area which is free to join but which contains high-profile adverts for a number of different products and services. IBM and Microsoft spent around $800,000 on Net advertising in 1996. Spending on Internet advertising rose by 83% in the first six months of 1996 to $71.1 million.

Advertising works on the knowledge that the average Net user looks at 200 pages a month, and many of those users are in upper income groups. Internet advertisers can be invoiced on the number of times a user selects their product pages. Each cluster of ten or a hundred visits then triggers another tiny amount onto the advertiser's bill. In this way advertisers know exactly what they are getting for their money.

130,000 new companies online in four months

Not surprisingly, every big company you could think of is clambering on the Internet band-wagon, or thinking of doing so. No less than 82% of corporate users aim to have their own server computers by the end of 1997, and people selling server facilities are expecting to earn at least $3 billion a year. Most of these new web-sites will provide far more than just an advertisement for their owners.

In addition, many companies which already have web-sites of their own are planning to expand them. This means yet more free gimmicks and useful ideas to draw us to their sites.

In the first four months of 1996 alone the number of major sites (domains) on the web rose from 170,000 to 300,000. This is a vast investment. Although it can vary enormously, the setting-up cost of some sites can be up to $1 million. Every site is now competing with the rest for attention, and the pressure is on to develop ever more interesting, entertaining and exotic features. This should hardly surprise us.

We need to recognise that the Internet is no longer the fringe activity of a few 'techno' types. On the contrary, it is having an impact on an ever increasing proportion of our society. Before long, most of the people in our churches and those whom we are trying to reach will have lifestyles influenced either directly or indirectly by the Internet.

And we need to realise that if cyberchurches are going to take off as a viable proposition (whether or not we approve of their existence), then they will probably do so by copying some of the Internet techniques already developed for buying and selling.

Hundreds of gadgets rolled into one

As well as the huge increase in power, another trend of future technology is the blurring of distinctions. We will see existing technologies redefining and expanding their roles to absorb the functions of other technologies, and the emergence of products which combine a whole range of functions simultaneously. Here are a few of the existing technologies that are likely to be affected by this trend:

Television (terrestrial)
Television (satellite/cable)
Interactive television

Video recorders/video libraries
Radio stations, including traffic information
Clocks
Message pagers
Mobile phones
Computers
Calculators
Navigation devices, e.g. satellite system in cars, with
  voice telling you which way to go at every junction
  over a 150-mile journey
Personal organisers

Entertainment stations to rival TV

Commercial terrestrial television is entirely financed by
brief adverts which fund long periods of technically high
quality television. Television companies are independent
of any advertiser, and sell space into programmes they
have already commissioned (with rare exceptions). However, on the Internet the operation is becoming reversed,
with major companies setting up their own entertainment
stations, looking to tempt Internet surfers into their area,
and hold them there long enough to keep hitting them with
adverts for their products. This is an all out war against
other Internet users and against conventional television.
The success of a campaign in future will be measured not
just by television ratings but also by millions of mouse
clicks.

So long as a company can be sure of attracting a big
enough number of participants (because Internet audiences like to be very interactive), then they might be
willing in time to cut their television advertising budget
and transfer it to Net entertainment. Internet users are a
prime target audience because of their relatively high
incomes, and because they are cutting down on television.

Perhaps as Christians we are already concerned about
the effect of new television channels, and the material
being broadcast by cable and satellite TV companies.

But the Internet may provide as many as 10,000 new TV channels within the next ten years, and certainly seems set to become the primary entertainment medium of the future. The implications of this are profound. We will look at the issue of content regulation later.

Success breeds success

Success breeds success, and the more millions of dollars are poured into free Net entertainment and information services, the more people will use the service and the more people will make purchasing decisions while there. At the same time, television companies are rising to the challenge, primarily by seeking to make their own technology interactive. This means that instead of simply watching television in a passive way, a viewer will be able to make choices between different options, to determine what direction the programme takes. Interactive TV gives power to the viewers, for example, to determine how characters behave in a soap opera, or even which article of clothing they take off next.

This concept is already here in a limited form with CD-ROMs where, from a given point, the viewer can move progressively through a series of options and choices in a branching pattern. The Internet could soon be the equivalent of having a library of 100,000 CD-ROMs at home.

At present, television provides moving images to a much higher standard than computers are currently capable of. But while TV companies seek to acquire the interactive dimension that is central to the Internet, the Internet, as we have seen, is rapidly moving towards the capacity to carry television, and to close that quality gap.

In five to ten years it may be very difficult to know whether you are enjoying interactive entertainment on a TV-quality computer system, or on a computer-powered television. In the middle of all this confusion will arrive large flat screens mounted across walls in rooms, providing high-resolution, wide-screen images and perhaps new three-dimensional projections.

The prospect of three-dimensional and interactive visual experiences will create a very exciting future if you enjoy new technology, a very nerve-wracking one if you are a television company, and certainly a disturbing one for Christians concerned about the potential abuses.

Television companies threatened by the future

I was talking to a friend the other day who is a regular television presenter for several programmes. He tells me that senior executives are now uncertain what television will even look like beyond 2000, let alone what sort of programmes people will want to watch once they have 500 or more channels to choose from – not including a billion Internet pages and tens of thousands of Internet videos to connect to.

Video rental shops on street corners are likely to take a real hammering and many will go out of business unless they find a new product by 1999. It may turn out to be something like ultra-high resolution interactive CDs, containing such vast amounts of interactive television and animation that even a cable system cannot compete. I doubt it somehow. Cable has huge untapped capacity, even without new systems to compress television transmission.

Internet telephone calls

It is not only TV companies that are facing pressure from the Internet. Another dramatic change, with huge implications for churches supporting missionaries around the world, is likely to be the widespread use of the Internet to make ordinary telephone calls. For some time Netscape has been distributing free trial software allowing people to speak to each other live while online. Several other companies have been doing the same.

I tried it out the other day. A computer user somewhere on the East Coast of the US got a surprise. He was busy working at his desk when a message flashed on his screen to say he was being called. A couple of seconds later he and I were in conversation. I have no idea who he was – I dialled a number at random from a list of people using the software, just to try it out. He was connected to the Net anyway and so was I in the usual way. There were no additional call charges. This is a frightening prospect for international telephone companies.

The quality of the call was poor, but we could understand each other most of the time once I had fiddled around with the settings. It made a mobile phone call sound like hi-fi, but then what do you expect when calling across the Atlantic for 1p a minute or less? In addition, we could exchange other data and work on things together using a shared screen. The very latest versions of these programs produce sound that matches telephone quality, provided there is sufficient modem speed.

Free international calls for up to twenty-four hours a day

Consider the economics. Suppose I live in London and I have an uncle in Auckland, New Zealand. First I sign up with a cable telephone company, which reduces my regular phone bills by around 10–15%. The company gives me unlimited free calls to all other cable subscribers in my area in the evenings and at weekends.

Next I sign up with an Internet provider at around $10 a month. I choose one that provides a no-frills service, with unlimited Internet use, day and night, for a year. My uncle has a similar arrangement, and also has a computer with modem, built-in microphone and speakers. At the pre-arranged time we both dial into the Internet and he waits while I contact him. He answers my call and we talk for as long as we like for no extra charge beyond the subscription fee of $10 a month.

I tried it out with a friend the other day. While we

were chatting he started sending me other things. Drawings started appearing on my screen. We were able to use the same screen and talk at the same time. Both computers began to operate as one. It was very strange at first.

Internet phone calls to ordinary phones

There are many other possibilities which are disturbing the chairmen of telecommunications companies. For example, there is little in practice to stop someone selling on to others a connection to an ordinary phone from his Internet computer, supplying a whole tower block with low-cost international calls at vast profit.

This is already happening. It is now possible to telephone anyone who has an ordinary phone, using your computer on the Internet. It is also possible for someone with an ordinary handset and a conventional phone line to dial you on your Internet phone. Finally, two people using ordinary phones in different countries can now be connected to each other via the Internet. Each dials a computer company which makes the connection – and a profit.

Many telecom companies are beginning to fight back, claiming a legal monopoly in many nations, with strict licensing rules. The trouble is that such rules are almost impossible to enforce, short of tracing and analysing every data transmission. In addition, consumers are likely to be unsympathetic once they wake up to the fact that the real costs to telecom providers of each call are almost zero once capital costs have been dealt with. Therefore the pressures will grow to provide far lower call costs or even free national calls in many countries, compensated for by slightly increased line rentals. The net result of all these changes is that we can expect to see far more dramatic falls in the price of ordinary telephone calls over the next few years.

Who pays the bill?

So who pays for all these Internet phone calls? The reality is that laying a fibre optic cable is very expensive, but flashing light pulses down it is virtually cost free. The same is true of satellites: placing them in space is hard work; operating them is automatic.

In some respects the telephone companies are doing rather well out of the Net if you multiply up all the hours spent connected. They also receive income from selling capacity on heavy duty connections between cities, paid for by Internet providers out of the money they in turn charge Internet users. And Internet providers can boost their own income by advertising.

So the reality of unlimited free access to the Internet is already here, even if live telephone and video quality is still erratic and poor. Despite the quality problems, around 500,000 have made Internet phone calls already, and 16 million people will probably do so by 2000.

Right now some Internet providers are trying to ban the use of phone links and video because just one or two people on the phone can use up as much capacity as twenty or more ordinary users. A key problem is that normal Internet traffic is carried a package at a time, and each package of a few written words is sent by the least busy route, literally hundreds of different ways around the world, sometimes passing through ten or more different computers to get from one place to another. If lines are busy, then the next part of a page, for example, may take a second or two longer to begin loading. This is fine for written text, but any appreciable delay in speech is unacceptable, as communication depends on instant or near instant response.

All these phone systems take advantage of a special Internet signal which demands priority over everything else. This means that telephone users can carry on completely unaware that the rest of the Internet is crashing all around the other local users. I have no doubt that these problems will be sorted out with added capacity, but in the meantime heavy users of video and speech could become very unpopular, or may find that they are charged more.

At times, as we have seen, the information highway is becoming like a motorway snarl-up, but experience shows that people don't stop using highways because of traffic jams; they just allow more time and campaign for road widening.

Mobile Internet telephones

As part of an Internet project for a major international corporation, I bought a Nokia 9000 Internet phone. This remarkable device looks like an ordinary phone but opens up to reveal a computer keyboard and screen. It is more powerful than many desktop computers bought as recently as three years ago. It is able to send and receive faxes (perfectly displayed), e-mail and short text messages. It can also be used to connect to the Internet, contains a full word-processor, diary, address book and most of the other functions of a personal organiser. It's really a perfect example of the next generation of computer devices. Is it a phone? Is it a computer?

It has had a revolutionary effect on my life in less than a month. While travelling on a train in Switzerland I was able to collect all my e-mail. I drafted replies to the urgent ones and sent them off. The total phone cost was three minutes. Then I resumed reading an important document I had downloaded from the Internet a few minutes earlier. During a meeting in London, a message flashed up on the screen. A few minutes later, having taken the call, I was standing on the Thames embankment writing a fax to the Press Association. I pushed a button, put the phone in my pocket and as I walked, copies of that fax were being sent all over the country.

Computer video links

Video cameras are likely to have a major impact on communications. I have one on my desk right now that is the size of an overgrown golf ball. The camera I have cost around £150 and produces clear black-and-white video. These amazing devices have nothing more than a thin wire coming out of the back of them, leading to a standard plug that inserts into the back of the computer. There is no computer card to insert. It can be used for two-way live video links (although picture change is slow) or to send video letters to people. I can leave video messages on people's e-mail answerphones. The camera is so small that I can hold it between finger and thumb and point it at whatever I want to show the other person – photos on my wall, a book I am reading or an illustration, or at the rest of my family if they also want to say 'hello'. Its image of me will be sent to anyone who calls for a video conference while I'm connected to the Net.

The other day I connected up to eight other people across the globe. I could see them all on my screen at the same time, and they could see me. The pictures were rather slow to change and we could only communicate by using keyboards, but by switching off all but one of the video links, enough capacity was freed for me to be able to have a 'telephone' conversation with someone in another continent, with quite reasonable sound quality. By switching off the video link to them as well, we were able to converse with near perfect sound quality. All this took place at the cost of a local call. As technology advances, quality will improve, and there will no longer be any need for the trade off between sound and vision.

These cameras can be plugged just as easily into a portable battery-operated computer. If such a computer is also online via a wire attached to a mobile phone, then someone in a car could have a video link with anyone else in the world.

Cameras will be as common as CD-ROMs

The technology is becoming so cheap that these cameras will one day be as standard as microphones, speakers and CD-ROMs, perhaps built into the computer screen on an adjustable mounting. It is rare today not to be offered multimedia options, and a fast modem is now part of many standard discounted packages. Cameras will be the next option to be included as manufacturers try their best to keep the average purchase price as high as before, despite the cataclysmic fall in prices of components. It is not worth a retailer selling a complex system for much less than £1,000, and this is why computers never seem to get as cheap as you think they should be – they just seem to become more powerful and gain more standard extras.

Cameras will be an attractive way for retailers to add back value, especially when they become fully detachable, battery-operated substitutes for ordinary 35mm film cameras as well. At present most such digital cameras do not function as video, nor the other way round, and digital still cameras are far more expensive than the low-quality golf balls. But changes are coming. The video golf balls already produce still pictures, albeit quite grainy, which can be used in web-pages or other resources.

A special guest for dinner on Christmas Day

Using the Internet as a cheap international phone service, especially with video images, opens up some interesting possibilities. It would allow, say, my uncle to join us for Christmas dinner. We just put the computer on the floor under the chair where he would have been sitting, and the screen and camera on a box on the chair. He can see us, and we can see him. We could be connected throughout a three-hour meal (provided we can get the time right for both of us), which he eats in New Zealand and we eat in London, all absolutely for free. He could even be eating exactly the same menu as us. We could toast each other's health. At the moment the images would be poor and some words would be lost from time to time, but cable modems or an ISDN would change all that. We could of course phone each other direct, but then I would be faced with an international call charge. And I would be tying up valuable phone lines full time.

In comparison, the Internet would make far more efficient use of the phone network, only sending packets of information when there is speech or video to send, and even then, only using spare capacity on hundreds of different lines as it arises, second by second, rather than hogging a whole line all the time. Thus several Internet users can be squeezed into the same capacity as one conventional user.

The potential in all this as a means for churches to provide support for missionaries working overseas is very significant, and we will come back to this.

Global church broadcasts to millions

For personal communication, all of these developments mean that the Internet is no longer limited to the cheap transmission of text messages for someone to read at a later time. The new technology opens up the way for direct real-time person-to-person communications using text, sound and video, all at very low cost. The next stage is to apply all this not only to one-to-one communications, but also to broadcasting. We've already seen global relays from rock concerts a number of times, and more recently in June 1996 Bill Gates of Microsoft gave a talk to 25,000 people simultaneously, all at their desks, on their own computer screens. This was especially significant because he used a video camera to provide images as well as sound. The same technology could be used to allow any computer user in the world with a modem to watch, say, a crusade where Billy Graham was speaking. Another taste of the future will be church broadcasts on a global scale via the Internet, with some tens of thousands or even millions listening in, all with the ability to interact too, asking questions, requesting information, contributing prayers.

Virtual reality

Virtual reality is another 'buzz' phrase very much associated with the Internet and a very controversial area for many Christians.

Virtual reality is a term used to describe the use of computers to create a completely artificial three-dimensional world, complete with buildings, trees, people, animals or whatever other objects take the fancy of those programming the system. The first VR systems were computer games, and programs used commercially to aid design.

There are two basic levels of VR. The first provides a picture on a flat screen of, say, a room in a house, but allows you to move around from room to room. What appears on your screen is identical to what would appear if someone were walking around holding a video camera. You can open doors, walk upstairs, look out of windows, go back down and outside into the garden. Although the images are no more three-dimensional than a television programme, the VR system is very useful commercially. For example, Sainsbury's recently wanted to redesign all their stores, and asked for a VR simulation. Directors could see exactly what it would feel like to walk down the redesigned aisles. Other examples have been in design and testing of equipment to be used in nuclear reactors, in deep sea diving, spacecraft and in medicine, training surgeons in the latest techniques using fibre optic instruments.

Three-dimensional world with sound, vision and touch

The second level of VR allows people to see everything in three dimensions. This can only happen by giving a slightly different image to each eye. The brain then interprets the differences in the two images to build a three-dimensional image identical to that seen in real life. One way to trick the brain is for the user to wear a headset with two tiny screens, worn like glasses inside a blacked-out cover so all visual contact is lost from outside. When stereo sound is added, the involvement of the user can be complete. If the user looks up or down, the picture changes, as it does if he or she moves to the left or right. More sophisticated systems include body fittings so that if, say, the person moves a hand, he or she sees a virtual image of the hand moving in an identical way.

Headsets, gloves and body suits

Special gloves and other equipment can provide a range of sensations to the user. In an advanced virtual reality world you can have the body of an athlete, be dressed in medieval armour and when you pick up a sword from the ground, you can even feel the hardness of the metal against your glove. As you look around, you can watch or talk with other people who are also in character – people who can see you – and you can even shake them by the hand. But these others might not be in the same room or the same building. They could be anywhere else in the world.

On-screen virtual reality also effective

At the moment such systems remain experimental, but a cruder version is already working on the Internet. The other evening my wife and I took a journey around a huge spaceship, opening doors, going in and out of lifts, up and down escalators, admiring the view of outer space – and also watching other people do the same. We went up to a few others and said 'hello' (text on screen).

On another occasion I met someone from Ontario in the spaceship, and someone else from another part of the world. There was no role play as such; we were all being ourselves. However the computer could not cope with three-dimensional real life photographs of each of us so we all had to choose a standard image from a large gallery. I chose the one that looked most like me. Some programs allow you to use your own three-dimensional image.

When you select a character you want to represent you in cyberspace, the three-dimensional Avatar picture in the gallery leaps out of the picture frame onto the middle of your screen and turns a full 360 degrees. Some people have a sense of humour and select bizarre appearances. In one room there was a large fish floating in mid air, talking to a dog!

We will look at the implications and possible dangers of all this in a later chapter. My purpose here is simply to describe what is already happening on the Net.

Building your own virtual world

On another occasion I visited a far bigger world. Unlike the spacecraft which was fully built and limited in size, this world is one great blank space. You arrive in the middle of what looks like vast countryside, with a few buildings dotted around. Every one of these has been designed and constructed by other inhabitants. For example, one person can claim part of a field and build a two-storey farmhouse, complete with furniture, carpets and other details. You can go inside and explore. Another person can build a road to another village and start building all along it. The screen displays are quite slow and you need huge amounts of memory for this system to work, but this is very early days.

Summary

The Internet will have a massive impact on the way we live. It will transform business, the entertainment world and personal communications. It may even create alternative realities. In doing so it opens huge dangers and immense possibilities both for society and for the church. As Christians we spend far too much time reacting to events. A look at a typical church office, with its limited and often obsolete equipment, betrays our attitude. We need long-range vision that takes us beyond even tomorrow's issues to prepare us for the future. The world is being rapidly carved up into two new halves: the information-haves and the information-have-nots. But the church needs to understand and reach both. The limitation is not cost. As we have seen, the cheapness of the Internet is one of its startling features. The issue, the challenge we must face up to, is our attitude to progress.

CHAPTER 3

The Character of the Internet

The sheer scale of the Internet may leave you feeling intimidated. Perhaps it sounds far too complex to grasp. And the speed of change and range of new possibilities highlighted in the last chapter may seem boggling. In this chapter we narrow the focus. What is it actually like to 'surf the Net'? And what sort of character does this electronic world have?

Search engines do the work

Most newcomers are surprised both by how easy it is to get started and how exciting it is. You might feel overwhelmed at the thought of 60 million pages, or 100 million or a billion beyond the turn of the century, but special software known as search engines is ingeniously designed to help you focus in on what you're looking for. The browser you use on the Internet has a 'search' button which activates these search engines. When you have found the sites or pages you want, your web browser can create a 'bookmark' so that next time you can go there straight away without having to search. Once you've found your favourite site you can stay there as long as you like.

Most regular users have several favourite areas where they spend most of their time, venturing out to find new things as needed. It appeals to the ancient hunter-gatherer instinct. If the site you are visiting has lots of information, with a couple of mouse clicks you can 'download' the information on to your own computer's hard disk and read it some other time. This also saves money on your phone bill.

For example, I was interested in the word 'cyber-church'. I typed it in and pressed 'enter'. Within four seconds the search engine had scanned 60 million pages of information from every continent and selected around 500 pages which specifically referred to cyberchurch. That's fast. In another three seconds I was already reading (and simultaneously printing out) pages on one of the world's first Internet churches, a congregation that never meets in the flesh and which has no buildings, but exists electronically with members from all over the world. In less than a second I had marked the page for future reference, adding it to my own personal library, now several hundred pages in size. Next time I was on the Net all I had to do was select the title I wanted using a cursor on the screen operated by a mouse, and almost instantly the same page appeared.

Hyperlinks flash across the world

Almost every page on the Net has words or phrases or pictures which come to life if selected. For example, a cyberchurch page might have the following sentence on it: 'This cyberchurch runs on a computer in Bethesda, Maryland. We have 250 MEMBERS and a LEADERSHIP TEAM of five. We meet on Sundays for WORSHIP. Drop in anytime.'

Clicking on MEMBERS, LEADERSHIP TEAM or WORSHIP will flash up extra information about those things. These hyperlinks can send you anywhere in the world, hopping almost at random from one area of interest to another.

Exhilaration . . .

Although I've tried to describe how it feels to sit down and use the Internet, there's really no substitute for direct experience. You have to try it for yourself. You could visit one of the 'cybercafés' springing up everywhere, or persuade a friend to let you have a go on their computer.

Many people find that when they overcome their initial uncertainty, there is often tremendous excitement. It's exhilarating to be linked to information coming from all over the world; to be able to jump from hyperlink to hyperlink according to your whim; to see the massive diversity of subjects covered so that there's always something of interest, always something new.

Many of the best pages use attractive graphic presentations, and may include artwork, photographs and, increasingly, sound and video clips. In its use of multimedia, the Net is like an exponentially growing CD-ROM, but with the difference that you can participate too: you can send messages, place orders, request information. As you gain experience you can create your own web-pages, using free software that takes a short time to learn, and make your message available to millions of other users. We'll talk about the potential in this for evangelism later on.

. . . And frustrations

The Internet is growing at a fantastic pace. Not only is the technology advancing rapidly, but the number of people using the web is also exploding. Sometimes there are problems when demand outstrips supply; and on any global network that is composed of thousands of different bits of equipment owned by different people, there are bound to be bottlenecks and breakdowns. You may find yourself 'crawling' the Internet rather than 'surfing', staring at a half-formed page on your screen waiting impatiently for the rest of it to arrive. This is especially the case at times of peak usage (daytime in the USA). If you have a slow modem, then receiving data-intensive pages with pictures, sounds and especially video clips can be a tedious business. You can get round this by upgrading your modem, or by setting your browser to receive text only. It seems likely though that for the foreseeable future there will always be a 'race' between ever growing demand and ever increasing supply as technology advances.

Other frustrations can occur in searching. Maybe the search engine throws up so many options that you don't know where to start; or perhaps none of the ones shown is quite what you are looking for. Sometimes you can't always tell from the search engine's summary whether the page will be useful, and you can have a trying time looking at likely pages that turn out to be irrelevant. With experience, you'll learn to define your search subject in a way that reduces this problem. Inevitably sometimes you will click on a hyperlink, only to find that the page you are looking for has moved or no longer exists; you'll simply receive an error message.

A way to reduce these frustrations and locate quality resources more painlessly, is to use reference lists created by someone else who is interested in the same things as you. Many organisations and individuals have done this. An example might be a site entitled 'A list of the best Bible study guides on the Internet'. You might consider publishing your own useful list. Internet magazines often have lists of particularly good reference points, and search engines such as Magellan only list reviewed sites which are given a star rating for usefulness.

Doesn't cost the earth

Many people assume that to be linked to the Internet, connecting to computers around the globe, must be a hugely expensive business. It certainly sounds as though it ought to be. In fact it isn't. Of course you need a computer with a modem to start with, but an increasing number of homes have computers anyway for work, leisure or children's education. Many people have access to computers at their workplace, and these days most church offices have a computer. The price of computers is steadily dropping, putting them within the budget of more and more people. Beyond this capital investment you will need to sign up with a service provider who provides your Internet access. Some of the popular service providers charge as little as £6 a month, plus an extra charge if you are on the Internet for long periods of time. Your service provider will probably be accessible by a local phone call. You may be accessing computer information from America, Singapore or Sydney, but you will only be paying local call charges.

Unlimited free information

An exciting feature of the Internet is free information. The reason for this is because the history of the Internet has been rooted in academic computer systems, with a strong philosophy that all knowledge should be free. Most of the 60 million pages of information available today can be read for free. Most of the programs are free – at least for a considerable trial period. Most of the photographs, sounds and video clips are free.

Radio broadcasts are also free. There are numerous radio stations around the world that are broadcasting through the Internet. To gain access to them you simply need to download software called *Real Audio* from the Net. As I write this sentence, I am in London listening to San Antonio Live Talk Radio (US). By using the Internet, radio stations can increase their audience at minimal cost in comparison to the station's overall budget. At the moment there is no Christian radio station on the Net as far as I am aware.

Giving knowledge away

Every conceivable group in our global society is now providing information. Pastors are making all their sermon notes available, scientists are making electronic versions of all their papers by uploading the text from their word-processor programs onto large computers linked to the Net. PhD students are publishing their entire doctorates, while children are publishing their own stories and poems. Companies are opening up their internal communications and governments are publishing millions of pages of official records. Airline timetables, weather charts, news bulletins, road maps, economic forecasts, investment information, exam revision guides – all sorts of things that one used to expect to pay for are now free.

The economics of it all are simple. It costs almost nothing to provide space for a few pages of text on a massive computer – a few pence a year, although you may be charged more. The costs of distribution are paid for by the charges made to people who have Internet accounts, and by telephone charges. The cost of collecting and writing the information can be considerable, but many copyright holders are prepared to waive any fees.

Authors may have little to lose

The loss of revenue is less than you may think. The biggest cost of most information is not writing or design, but production and distribution. For example, the author of a book typically earns far less than 10% of the official sale price of the book when published. All the rest is lost along the way in order to get the book into your hands. That book may only sell a few hundred copies or a few thousand anyway. The total financial yield for an author of a paperback may in fact be quite modest. The yield for an article or booklet or set of lecture notes may be even less.

Many information providers like the thought of large numbers of people using their material more than the thought of very few doing so and their being a small amount richer. Most writers write because they have an inner compulsion rather than purely for money. It's not surprising that tens of thousands of people have already turned to publishing their work on the Net.

A new home for old newspapers and books

There is another reason: most commercial information has a limited shelf-life. Newspapers cannot be sold after a day, nor magazines after a month, while books only remain on the shelf so long as they keep selling in reasonable numbers. Old information is commercially worthless – not because no one in the world wants to read it, but because the costs of conventional distribution outweigh the amount people are prepared to pay for it. Another reason it is commercially worthless may be that a small target audience scattered in different countries may be completely unaware that the resource exists, and it would cost too much to advertise.

Therefore there is little or no lost income from donating old material to other Net users. It is true that some specialist providers like Reuters can charge a large amount for people to be able to search for subjects among back issues of around 2,000 publications, but that is a highly specialised service.

Who is using the Net?

A key factor in understanding the character of the Net is knowing something about the people who are using it. I often hear people say that only computer nerds and 'sad people' use the Net. How wrong they are. Almost four out of ten homes in the US already have a personal computer and one in three of these has a modem enabling the computer to be connected to the telephone lines. By the year 2000, less than three years away, at least 20% of all US households are expected to be online.

At present the median age of users is thirty-two years, 64% have college degrees and 25% have an income larger than $80,000 (£50,000), so the image of the long-haired student computer freak is quite wrong. Half of Internet users have managerial or professional jobs and 31% are women. If the church is interested in reaching well-educated middle-class men, then the Internet is an obvious way to do it.

For every home user there are one or two others who use the Net primarily at work. They use it for e-mail, to receive up-to-date financial information, for writing reports, for research and also for entertainment during work breaks. The Net has moved from being primarily a university tool to a major source of commercially valuable information.

More than forty hours a week online

The Internet is having a direct impact on people's lifestyles and creating a new unreached people group. One survey of men in New York found that around one in five spent forty hours or more a week on the Net, while 62% spent more than two hours a week on it. The average weekly use by men and women was 6.5 hours. Six out of ten said that they had cut down on television as a result, with some pundits predicting that Internet use could exceed television audiences at prime time in some US cities.

Internet addiction is becoming a medically recognised problem with signs of irritability following withdrawal. Some people get a huge buzz out of zipping around the world via their computers. Internet use increases arousal and probably releases endorphins as well as other hormones related to stress. We will look at cyberaddiction later.

How Christian is the Net?

With such dramatic growth in every conceivable source of information, from millions of different places, it is hardly surprising that religion is also a growing presence on the Net. Every religious group imaginable is now represented in one way or another, all competing for the attention of the 40 million already connected. Contributions range from official pronouncements by the leaders of religious organisations, to propaganda of various types, to the incoherent ramblings of individual fanatics. All are indexed automatically so that when you enter a word like 'Hinduism' or 'Christianity', a full selection appears in around four seconds.

So how Christian is the Internet? Is the image of computer-mad technokids and sex-obsessed college students justified? It took me just a few minutes to do a survey of the contents of some 60 million pages. By the time you read this, I expect that number will have more than doubled. What is interesting is the relative sizes of the Internet libraries on various topics. Christianity is quite high on the list, with around 300,000 pages – far higher than any other religion.

Here are the results of my survey using a search facility called Alta Vista. I used some common words, and also tried some books of the Bible and some denominations. You may conclude that none of us needs Christian reference libraries any more.

Number of times the following words appear (approx.)		Number of documents
Christian	736,569	300,000
Jesus	515,747	100,000
Bible	301,606	100,000
Catholic	210,535	90,000
Baptist	112,271	40,000
Christianity	81,051	40,000
Methodist	75,549	30,000
Lutheran	64,276	20,000
Theology	41,251	20,000
Worship	39,402	20,000
Seminary	38,196	10,000
Protestant	27,194	10,000
Salvation	24,155	10,000
Evangelical	21,482	10,000
Anglican	16,319	9,000
Resurrection	14,530	9,000
Redemption	12,843	8,000
Baptism	12,256	6,000
Apostles	11,980	6,000
Deuteronomy	8,667	4,000

Pentecostal	8,043	4,000
Evangelism	7,813	4,000
Leviticus	6,223	2,000
Discipleship	3,350	2,000
Charismatic	3,263	1,000
Philemon	2,791	1,000
Episcopalian	1,986	1,000
Propitiation	122	93
Colossians	11	9

For comparison (in order):

Satan	89,289	30,000
Islam	87,614	
Hindu	40,864	10,000
Buddhism	37,842	10,000
Judaism	33,741	10,000
Mormon	29,025	9,000
Mohammed	16,975	10,000
Confucianism	3,694	2,000

Christianity is the dominant religion of cyberspace

The low score for Islam is a reflection of the US bias of the Net which is strongly dominated by Christianity when it comes to religion. Christian allegiance is growing worldwide at an extraordinary rate, with 33% of all those alive today, increasing at 2.7% per year – far faster than the growth in world population, which is a mere 1.7%. However, Islam can count 20% of the world as its adherents, increasing even faster at 2.9% per year. Despite this huge following, Mohammed is mentioned just 17,000 times compared to Jesus, who clocks up no fewer than 515,000 references.

It is also interesting to see how the Christian faith measures up against computers, money and sex on the Net, in terms of the number of documents mentioning particular key words. This is a crude measure but gives us a rough guide to the sort of material people are placing on the Net in relative quantities. However, it gives no indication of actual page use or traffic to those sites.

Christianity pages are as many as for sex

Comparisons over numbers of documents containing (approx.) 60 million pages:

America	1,000,000
Money	800,000
UK	700,000
Computers	600,000
IBM	600,000
Law	500,000
Christian	300,000
Electronics	300,000
Sex	300,000
Television	200,000
Politics	200,000
China	200,000
Crime	60,000
Olympics	40,000
Uganda	10,000

So then, Christianity probably has as many pages devoted to it on the Internet as sex, and three times more than any other world religion.

Christian publishers in cyberspace

There are major prospects here for the Christian publishing and music industry, especially in the US, but not necessarily based in the US. The Internet is so global that it does not matter at all where the actual retail outlet is physically. The CD sound samples can still be listened to and instant electronic orders placed. Despatch costs and times may be slightly greater, but that is all.

This has two consequences. First, a major Christian

publisher (or wholesaler) of books, magazines and music could set up in the US, and after selling primarily to the US market could then start targeting other countries very heavily. Secondly, a company could set up an Internet presence based somewhere such as the UK, once again aiming for the huge US Christian retail market, while also picking off other English-speaking nations. Whoever takes the major lead is likely to gain and keep a big slice of the action. Not surprisingly, this possibility has caused much concern in the publishing industry, where international selling agreements are open to abuse that is far harder to detect, since no geographical or political barriers exist between supplier and customer.

Christian presence will grow fast

Since many parts of the church have hardly even begun to think about serious use of the Internet, and many individual believers are still very cautious about it all, it seems clear to me that we are likely to see a huge surge of Christian influence on the Net over the next few years. As we will see, the Internet offers great advantages to churches and Christian organisations in a number of areas. With all these options, high speed and low cost are important factors compared to other ways of achieving the same things. Section 2 looks at how the church can seize the potential of the Internet.

Summary

Many people are cautious, even fearful, of the Internet. They feel that its size and speed of growth are overwhelming. They perceive it as too costly and difficult to use, and irrelevant to their lives. Many see cyberspace as a dangerous place to be, following media concentration on the Internet as a haven for pornography and subversive activity.

In reality, the cost of Internet connection has plummeted, and it is very easy to use – in fact many people find it exhilarating. And, contrary to popular belief, most Net users are responsible professional people in higher income brackets.

The scale of the impact that the Internet will have on our society compels us, as Christians, to be at the forefront of change. Happily, the Net already has a strong Christian presence. It is true that unhealthy material also exists on the Net, but surely this should only be a provocation to greater Christian involvement, not withdrawal. As it is said: 'Evil flourishes when good men stay silent.'

Seizing the Potential

CHAPTER 4

Cyberlinks Overseas

Bridging the gap

Most churches of any size have a number of workers overseas whom they are endeavouring to support, but support means more than just financial help. Life in many parts of the world can be extremely isolating for missionaries, with many daily problems to face ranging from vehicle breakdowns to ill health and spiritual exhaustion. The Internet can help.

You might think that those in the poorest nations would be furthest behind in embracing new technology, and that the Internet would be wholly inappropriate in a country with intermittent electricity and creaking telephone systems. You may be in for a surprise. Electronic mail is a runaway success, becoming a vital lifeline when communication is poor.

Internet more reliable than mail or fax

In 1988 I was in Uganda on a ministry trip, speaking about a Christian response to AIDS and talking to church leaders about what could be done to care for people and save lives. Since then a major Christian work has been established. One of the frustrations was that during the civil war many of the telephone cables and junction boxes were buried, to thwart attempts by soldiers to cut lines. But when it rained, which it often did, water would flood the connectors and the lines would go down. At other times the electricity supply would fail. Things have improved, but in many other developing nations there are similar problems.

Fax machines have speeded up communication enormously, delivering mail reliably up to ten days before it would otherwise arrive. However, you can only receive or send a fax with both power and a working telephone line. Fax is also expensive in international telephone costs and in paper. Since faxes fade quite rapidly in hot climates, there are also added photocopying costs.

The alternative is e-mail, which is becoming practical now that access to computers is more widespread. Incidentally, second-hand computer prices have now reached the point where a machine costing several thousand pounds six or seven years ago can be bought for a couple hundred or less. Yet it may be in reasonably good order and be just as capable of running all the programs it ran on the day it was bought. Repairs may not be too costly if there are a number of such machines around which can be cannibalised for spares. Often it is just a question of swapping boards or disks over until the machine works again.

E-mail saves missions money

E-mail has advantages in terms of both cost and reliability. Once the equipment has been bought, sending a long e-mail is likely to cost a fraction of the cost of a fax because of the speed of transmission. Likewise, receiving e-mail onto a disk is far cheaper and faster than printing onto fax paper. To give you some idea: an entire copy of this book would probably take only a few minutes to download. A good e-mail program allows you to write a stack of letters to different people, with added documents as necessary.

When you next connect to the network, all the mail is automatically delivered in a few seconds to the nearest big computer, which automatically sorts and sends it, while also sending back any fresh mail received. The computer can log on and off in less than a minute, making a longer distance connection still reasonably practical.

Sending Internet pages via e-mail

A friend of mine in Zimbabwe has an e-mail account in Johannesburg, some distance away, yet he is still saving a small fortune by using e-mail wherever he possibly can. It has revolutionised his life, even though e-mail is all he has. He cannot call up web-pages. All he can do is send and receive mail.

He is hoping to be connected to the Internet one day, but in the meantime we are talking about ways in which I could set up a system to extract interesting web-pages and e-mail them to him. If a big cluster of pages was sent he could load them all onto his hard disk and read them with a browser. In this way all the hyperlinks should work perfectly, so long as they point to other pages in the set I send him. He could end up with an instant interactive teaching module which everyone on the mission could use as part of their training.

Week by week, with the addition of new pages and updates of old ones, his hard disk could become more and more useful as a huge collection of related Internet pages on health and development. He would have his own subset of the Net, a 'mini-Net' of his own, that he could use at any time without any connection charges.

We have yet to try it out and we may be overtaken by the arrival of low-cost Internet access in the city where he lives, but these discussions are typical thinking among many others all over the world who are also looking to join the information highway from developing nations.

My friend can receive e-mail now from any country. It is safely held until the next time the computer is turned on with electric power and a working telephone line. No more waiting due to engaged or unobtainable tones by those trying to reach him. No more waiting for a long fax to churn through. No more frustrations with error messages with half-received faxes. No more delays with expensive 'snail mail'. These are some of the reasons why it is so common to find field workers in poorer nations who are more familiar with e-mail than some of their colleagues at head office in wealthy industrialised cities.

E-mail is now available quite widely, but full World Wide Web Internet access is still both limited and expensive in developing countries. This will change soon, particularly in Africa where a major initiative is underway to bring full Internet access to most larger cities, backed by international aid.

Churches should consider e-mail for overseas links

Church supporters should seriously consider using e-mail to help shorten the distance from home for missionaries who are feeling isolated and vulnerable. Church newsletters can easily be sent, in addition to personal letters, along with a host of other encouraging material.

For those with access to the Internet there are some exciting options to consider, ranging from Internet Relay Chat, through to telephone and video links. Incidentally, those not on the World Wide Web can still receive video e-mail letters, where a two- or three-minute video message is recorded and sent, although this process may take ten to fifteen minutes. They can also receive any web-pages you have downloaded for them.

Many newsgroups have an e-mail facility so that all new postings by different people are sent automatically to the e-mail boxes of those who request to receive the service. Postings can also be made via e-mail. Therefore any e-mail user in a developing country should be able to be a full and active participant in these forums.

Chatting on the Net using a keyboard

As we have seen, Internet Relay Chat is a rather primitive communication tool but it could be a lifesaver for a depressed and homesick worker several thousand miles away. All it needs is a standard computer and a modem connected to the Internet. Microphones, speakers and cameras are not used.

The two users (and as many dozens of others as wish to) are linked by a common message board which appears on all their screens. Whatever anyone types is seen simultaneously against their name by everyone else, letter by letter as the text is entered. Although there is no sound or picture, the feeling of proximity can be very intense, profound and comforting. Of course it is far cheaper than an international telephone call. It works best if the people communicating can type reasonably well. The following is an example.

John is in Buenos Aires, but is an old friend of Peter and Mary, a couple who were a part of the same church back home in Newcastle, but are themselves now living in Uganda. Richard is a member of the leadership team of the Newcastle church. This is how the conversation would appear line by line. I have also been invited to listen in.

Richard: Hello, anyone there?

John: Hi there from Buenos Aires.

Peter: I'm here. Mary's here. Hello, John.

John: I'm sorry, Peter, to hear Caroline had malaria. How is she?

Peter: Recovering. It was a bad shock. Last week was the worst.

Richard: We had all the church praying for you last Sunday night.

John: All of our mission have been praying for you too.

Peter: Thanks. The others here have been great.

Patrick: Hi there, Peter.

Peter: Thanks for coming online . . . I needed to ask you a question about the malaria tablets and side-effects . . .

Summary

Communication with Christian workers overseas often acts as an emotional, mental and spiritual lifeline for them. It is a high priority that communication should be as effective as possible. Compared to e-mail and Internet Relay Chat, faxes are slow and costly; mail is slow and unreliable; telephones are expensive, provide no hard copy of the communication, and have the problems of time zones and inconvenience if the worker is not at the phone. Internet communication is cheap, fast and flexible, allowing documents, training materials, etc. to be transmitted at the same time as a message of greeting. Establishing Internet links should be a high priority for churches and Christian organisations with workers overseas.

CHAPTER 5

Cyberevangelism

A great opportunity

The Internet represents a massive evangelistic opportunity. It is estimated that 40 million people are currently connected to the Internet, and this is expected to grow rapidly. To have access to a potential audience of this scale is an evangelist's dream. We have the best news in the world, and we now have a new way of communicating it. Because the Internet is so difficult to regulate, it opens up the potential for evangelistic witness into countries that are hostile to the gospel and will not admit missionaries or Bibles.

Closer to home, the majority of Internet users are professional men, a group that the church has found difficult to penetrate with much success. One of the great attractions of Internet evangelism is that you are communicating directly into someone's own home. This means that those who are not yet Christians can make enquiries with the security of anonymity, and the ability to disconnect whenever they wish. In contrast to face-to-face evangelism, it also means that they can take in our message at a speed they can manage rather than at the speed we present it to them; they can read short sections of a Christian page, for example, and ponder it for a few days before returning for more. So far, because of the poor level of understanding about the Internet among Christians, and a general sense of caution, the potential is still largely untapped. Just what means can we use to make the most of the opportunities?

Usenet groups, newsgroups

These are online debating forums, numbering several thousand and covering every conceivable subject, including a large number of groups covering Christianity, religion, spirituality and philosophy. The quality of contribution to these discussion groups varies from the considered and thoughtful, to the cynical, superficial, offensive and blasphemous. Yet among all the rubbish you will find comments by people with genuine questions about the Christian faith who want an open and frank debate. Sadly the response has often been of poor quality. A number of those believers who have engaged in the process have lacked the skills to be effective.

Take care before intruding

I am not sure how ethical it is to attempt to control or manipulate other forums that are nothing to do with faith issues, and to attempt to use them as platforms for presenting the gospel. I am all for getting involved everywhere and for taking every opportunity that exists to explain the hope that is within us, but you will quickly antagonise other Net users if you breach established protocols.

You may even risk being 'bombed' by thousands of computer generated rubbish messages. Since your e-mail box has a limited capacity, this can render it useless for several weeks. Such things are quite common. Another breach of ethics is to send unsolicited e-mail, or to place identical contributions in several different newsgroups or bulletin boards.

However, sometimes Christians are nicer than Jesus was himself. I cannot see any reason against complaining about people who post blasphemous and obscene messages onto Christian sites. In my view, such Net users should not be surprised if they find several hundred different Christians have become so fed up by the intrusions that they have all sent a message of objection to the author's own mailbox. That should be enough to dissuade most people. Many newsgroups are moderated, which means that offensive contributions are not added, nor ones which simply repeat points already raised by others. There is nothing to stop a group of Christians from setting up their own, perhaps looking at key questions raised by those looking into the Christian faith.

E-mail can open doors

As we have seen, most Internet users at present are men and many men are notoriously bad at writing letters, yet a considerable number find e-mail less formal and are comfortable with sending messages back and forth on a computer. Writing e-mail messages can take place during a break time when a person is already at the computer. They are cheaper than phone calls (especially if going overseas), and don't suffer the problem of the recipient being engaged. The recipient can access the e-mail at their convenience, produce a hard copy of it if required, and take time to frame a response, all of which are advantages compared to the phone.

As a result, lengthy exchanges can result which would be quite unthinkable with pen and paper, on all kinds of important issues. I know a local minister who has found that e-mail correspondence with his two brothers has opened up new depths in their relationships and excellent opportunities to discuss spiritual matters. If the person is reasonably local it might even be possible to invite him to a meeting of some kind, or to meet up when travelling in that direction, or to put him in touch with believers in his area.

Web-sites

The World Wide Web provides an excellent medium for evangelism in that it allows the gospel to be communicated in fresh, exciting ways, using images, video clips and sounds, and with the possibility for participation and interaction. Hyperlinks can take the surfer to any number of related pages on different subjects or other Christian sites. This increases the chances that the surfer will find something that hooks them, even if the first page does not. In most forms of evangelism, the evangelist carries the responsibility of judging the best approach; with web-based evangelism, the not-yet-believer is allowed to set the agenda, to scratch where they are itching, and this can be very fruitful. It allows the not-yet-believer to be actively involved. Too much conventional evangelism imposes an essentially passive role on them. Interestingly, Jesus himself often used this approach, teaching in response to people's questions.

Internet Alpha

Alpha courses have had a major evangelistic impact in recent years. Why not an Internet Alpha course? This could combine the different facilities of the Internet. An attractive multimedia Alpha web-site based on the notes from the talks would be the main contact point. E-mail and IRC would allow the person accessing the course to engage in dialogue. As technology advances, of course, it would be possible for tens of thousands around the world to see and hear the Alpha course session as it happened. Indeed, as we have seen, this is already possible for those with fast modems.

A mouse click away from oblivion

A challenging aspect of web-evangelism is the need to engage the 'surfer'. The Internet evangelist is only one mouse click away from oblivion. The surfer doesn't have to get you out of the door, make polite excuses or sit through to the end, or worry about offending you. Evangelists have always had to try and communicate the gospel in ways that are relevant, attractive and comprehensible, but on the Internet there is that much less margin – you can't afford to be less than ruthlessly good at it.

Sadly, although there are quite a large (and rapidly increasing) number of Christian web-sites, a fair proportion of them are of mediocre quality or rather maverick in style. Furthermore, many of the better quality sites are written for the Christian community rather than evangelistic. It would be tragic indeed if we allowed this great opportunity to pass by, and merely created an electronic ghetto of Christians huddled together with their backs to the world.

What type of web-site works?

Most use of the Internet by churches so far has been fairly unimaginative and has consisted largely of a front page giving general information about the church, plus a copy of the church logo, with supplementary pages on church activities, leadership profiles and other information. The displays are often badly illustrated and are completely static, without any updated information. These sites are the equivalent of entries in a denominational handbook and as such do have a value, especially for visitors to an area. Better presented sites take time to prepare and one needs to be sure of a cost benefit – especially to a church with very modest resources.

For example, my own church, Bridge Church in West London, was offered some web-space on a site run by our mother church, from which we were planted five years ago. Their own pages are well laid out, with information about the church and local information about the area, places to eat, sights to see. Anyone typing 'Ealing' will find Ealing Christian Fellowship comes high up on the index list. Thus anyone typing 'Ealing restaurants' will also find themselves in the church web-site.

We quickly threw together a few paragraphs about ourselves to go on the same site. It is enough to enable people to find out where we meet, and some have. Now we are considering a larger presence, perhaps even a web-site of our own. Ealing Christian Fellowship's web-space was in turn a gift from a church member who had more space than he needed. Incidentally, after a few months, Ealing Christian Fellowship had their first new person coming along as a direct result of the web-site alone. He was an Internet enthusiast who was moving into the area, and was impressed by the only church who was Internet-aware.

How to attract visitors

The next stage on from this is to provide a service so that large numbers of people are drawn to the site. The service could provide regularly updated information of various kinds, or valuable, interesting, fun or unusual information attracting visitors. The obvious information to update would be church news, details of events coming up and other information. This is unlikely to be a cost-effective exercise unless there is someone in the church who loves playing with computers, or unless the church is of some size with a congregation where a significant number of people use the Net.

The second avenue is to provide a stack of useful information unrelated to the church, but for which the church gains credit and free advertising. In such a case the larger and more varied the site is the better. Ealing Christian Fellowship's first steps have been an experiment along this route, but far more can be done.

A good example is that of City Gate Church in Southampton, in conjunction with the church from which it had been planted. They launched a web-site in September 1995 aimed at university students. They advertised it through beer mats based on the Guinness advert slogan 'Pure Genius', and in newspapers. They also registered with the main Internet search engines.

The response was very positive. The audience mainly consisted of students, all of whom had free access via the university server. During term time the site has been busy. E-mail has been more successful than the slow web-site they had for distributing weekly news. They asked students to register their e-mail addresses – more reliable than their constantly changing postal addresses.

As a church with around 120 adults, over a year they have seen seventy students come along on a fairly regular basis, all of whom are on e-mail, plus a further fifty or so who are also on the list. It took Mike Santer, part of the leadership team, around four days to create the site, and some time since keeping it up to date. Using e-mail meant that less time needed to be wasted resetting the web-site pages.

Penetrating anti-Christian nations

Cyberspace contains not only people who are in industrialised nations, spending more and more of their social time on the Net, but also others in anti-Christian nations whose only contact with Christian thinking may be through the Net. An example of a targeted approach to cyberevangelism might be to finance and set up a large Arabic web-site with a number of interesting discussion/activity areas, but which also provides debating forums on faith issues and related matters, including an 'introducing Christianity' area. Who knows, it could lead to an online Arabic Alpha course, introducing the basics of the Christian faith. One interesting feature of IRC and the Internet in general, is that the identity and appearance of the person is unknown at the start. This could be an advantage in cross-cultural work where only written words are used, and there are no artificial barriers created by accent or the colour of skin.

What are the real costs?

Developing big, well-illustrated sites is expensive in terms of time and resources, although the costs in cash terms are very low indeed. Some service providers offer up to ten megabytes of space included in the monthly subscription. Ten megabytes is enough to contain up to thirty different paperbacks this size (text only). However, the space rapidly disappears if large graphics are used.

Even quite modest investments can pay dividends. One local minister I know has set up an evangelistic site which is less than a megabyte in size. His congregation consists of only thirty-four people, and together with his friends his 'circle of witness' is less than 100, but in the last few months alone his Internet site has been visited by over 12,000 people, a number of whom have sent him e-mails inviting further dialogue.

Nevertheless, the best sites are 'state of the art', containing all the latest gizmos such as sound and video, animation and exceptional layout and design, all combined with very well-written text. There are some superbly thought out Christian sites around, examples of which are listed at the back of this book. One way to develop a good site is to explore and copy interesting features. It is possible to download a page and use the codes to generate a similar layout, inserting your own graphics and text. The final result will be totally different, but the quality may be far more professional.

Recognising the limitations

While the church needs to act more quickly to seize the opportunities, it's important that we don't get too carried away into unrealistic expectations. Internet evangelism has some limitations that we should be aware of. First, although there may be millions of people using the Net, it's another thing to get their attention. The Internet evangelist will be a small voice amid a great clamour of noise, competing for attention with high-spending companies and large organisations.

Secondly, web-sites are essentially impersonal. Statistics indicate that personal relationships are the most effective form of evangelism. Nevertheless, evangelistic web-sites may prove valuable as pre-evangelism, the sowing of seeds, establishing credibility which provokes someone to make contact with a local church, or at least to make an e-mail enquiry.

Problems of follow-up?

Some may argue that there is no point in talking to people in such a remote way when there is so little prospect of follow-up. But what about Philip and the Ethiopian in Acts 8:26–40? Why did the angel of the Lord call Philip down that desert road? There was little time for teaching, no chance of follow-up. This was a God-given encounter – humanly speaking an unplanned event – yet it had eternal purpose and meaning.

Anyway, perhaps the Internet is less impersonal than we might think. Christian web-sites can (and should) include an e-mail address to encourage enquiries, which opens up the possibility of more personal communication. After all, if people are meeting through IRC on the Net, and then falling in love and getting married, it is obvious that what is happening here has greater potential than you might imagine from the cold description of it. It is extremely hard to explain in rational words why these electronic communications should be so powerful – but they are. As the church wakes up to the potential of the Internet, it will increasingly be possible to direct enquirers to churches close to where they live.

The limits of persuasion

Even where we endeavour to make Internet evangelism more personal, there's no escaping the fact that it is still essentially indirect. The main focus of Internet evangelism has to be persuasion since there is very little opportunity for demonstration of the gospel. Seeing and experiencing the gospel at work in people's lives is probably the most effective form of witness. People need to see Christians in times of stress, in their homes, with their children, dealing with other people's needs, worshipping, praying for the sick. People are powerfully touched by the way they are received into a Christian home or meeting, by the atmosphere of love and fellowship, by the miracles great and small that take place when the Holy Spirit is at work. All of these things are largely precluded by the Internet. This would be the major limitation of an Internet Alpha. The success of these courses has been built around personal relationships and an experience of the presence of God. This is not to say that God cannot visit someone where they sit at their computer, but merely to observe that in general he prefers to act in a relational context.

The question of trust

The Internet is a computer activity, technological and scientific. Although it's too early to say yet, it is conceivable that people will feel suspicious of a link between technology and spirituality. This might be based on a sense that religion should be linked to tradition – people are sometimes attracted to churches because they want to rediscover lost values. The highly publicised moral failures of TV evangelists may heighten suspicion of religion experienced indirectly through a screen.

A private world

By communicating through a screen in a person's own home, there is a danger that Internet evangelism will reinforce Western culture's concept that spirituality belongs to the realm of the private and personal rather than the public and corporate; something that can be switched on and off at will. This serves as a reminder that the prime goal of Internet evangelism, as with any other type of evangelism, is not merely to make converts but to make disciples who acknowledge the lordship of Christ in every aspect of their lives, and who understand what it means to be members of the body of Christ, joined together. Personal relationship building will always be at the heart of evangelism, and Internet evangelism will be at its most effective when it builds a bridge to this person-to-person experience of the kingdom of God.

The need for training

Given the enormous potential of Internet evangelism, we need to ask: Where are all the cyberevangelists? Where are the people with excellent written communication skills and keyboard skills who could make a real impact? There are too many mavericks in there at the moment. No doubt many of them are very well meaning, but they are not providing the quality one would hope for. Having said this, they are the only ones in many cases who have bothered to be involved at all. They have forged ahead despite huge apathy from many church leaders and training colleges.

Hidden resources

Internet evangelism requires many different skills found in the more conventional approaches. A great deal has been invested over the years in training people for face-to-face evangelism, including streetwork, door-to-door activity and other things, so why don't we start training in cyberevangelism? Perhaps there are people in our churches who lack the gifts and confidence for effective face-to-face evangelism, and whom we tend to overlook. But many of them may have a mature faith, and could easily be given keyboard skills if they don't have them already. They might never dream of being able to talk to a stranger on the street, yet could be highly effective talking to someone on IRC or through a newsgroup from the other side of the world or the other side of town. There's no reason why Christians who are housebound or limited physically in other ways could not develop a significant evangelistic ministry in this way.

Summary

Internet evangelism is a key area. Cyberspace contains a major unreached people group (which, incidentally, is under consideration to be included in Patrick Johnstone's excellent book *Operation World*). The potential audience is immense, and includes many people whom conventional evangelism is finding hard to reach. It holds the possibility of bringing the gospel to places where conventional evangelism is barred. We should see it as an exciting addition, not as a substitute for existing approaches to evangelism. Our aim should be to ensure that unbelievers contacted through Net evangelism are linked into direct personal relationships with other Christians local to them. We need to recognise the potential, and to see that it demands a completely new strategy, new programmes, new training, new systems of follow-up, new methods of discipleship. There may be people in our churches who are overlooked for conventional evangelism but would be a great resource for these new opportunities.

CHAPTER 6

Cyberteaching

A teaching resource

The Internet has great power as a teaching resource and many churches are now beginning to explore this. It is one thing just to provide an advertising service or an information newsletter or information for enquirers, but how about training courses on the Net, discipleship courses, theology study and leadership development?

The great strength of the Net is interactivity so that learning can be precisely tailored to the progress of the individual. In that sense Internet-based training is no different at all from a standard computer-assisted education programme of some kind. However, programs on CDs or disks involve large production costs, and enormous amounts of time can be wasted installing software, only to find that it has limited compatibility with existing systems.

The Internet avoids all these problems and allows for immediacy, so that all those using the course materials have instant access to any changes made. This is particularly important in studying topics where information can go out of date, such as the Christian response to ethical issues, where the latest court case or news headline could form part of the lesson.

Flexible Bible school

The potential of the Internet as a means for a new approach to training is already being explored by a company called BestLinks in Bristol. *Best Academy* is a 'virtual school' which allows students to enrol on courses from anywhere in the world, using the Internet. Their study materials are sent over the Internet by file transfer so that they can work offline in their own time. The study materials can of course include Internet links to other resources. When students complete assignments they are sent over the Net to the school, which forwards them to the tutor for assessment. The tutors can be based anywhere in the world. The tutor's comments, together with the next module's materials, are then returned to the student.

Distance learning is not new in itself, of course. Its great flexibility for students and tutors alike is already recognised. But by using the Internet, the cost of producing, updating and sending materials is greatly reduced, the materials themselves can be attractively multimedia, and communication is greatly accelerated. As we have seen, new technology will create the possibility of students having audio-visual tutorials, removing one of the current limitations of existing distance learning.

A gateway to the Third World

Surprisingly Internet access has grown rapidly even in poor countries. This opens up a huge new market for Christian training materials. In the past, indigenous churches, struggling with poverty, have simply not had the resources to buy books and other materials which are costly to publish and expensive to transport around the world. The Internet opens up the possibility for regularly updated resources to be sent at a fraction of the cost. Each person in the host nation who is Internet connected can act as a distribution point to scores of others in their churches. The SOON Gospel Literature organisation (a part of WEC International) is distributing materials in just this way, and has also created a web-site specifically designed to attract people who are learning English in overseas countries. It is excited by the potential to access nations that have been restrictive. And of course this is not only one-way traffic:

the Internet allows Christians in poor nations to educate Western Christians too.

Good ideas will continue to develop

As course organisers become familiar with the Internet, and compare what they have created with what is on offer elsewhere, their ideas are likely to become more ambitious. A training course consisting merely of a plain set of text pages in January might have expanded into a well-illustrated lecture by May, and become a fully interactive sound and video learning experience by December. While all the capability for these things may well have been available from the start, familiarity with the techniques needed, ideas about design, and limitations of computer hardware all encourage continuous innovation rather than one big leap.

Internet teaching could allow us to select any one of a hundred thousand ministry tapes by all kinds of preachers and teachers, alive or dead, from different countries of the world. One is hardly likely to be overwhelmed by the choice, since each set of, say, ten to twenty tapes would only be presented in response to a search. Thus a search for Baptist teaching on the nature of the church might yield a very different result from a list of tapes on euthanasia or Christian political action, or 1940s tapes on pacifism.

Multimedia allows lecture notes to be highlighted on the screen as a pre-recorded talk proceeds, or for the listener to view a photograph of the speaker – or perhaps a full video. As with a CD-ROM, an Internet talk can be instantly started, stopped or restarted at any point the listener chooses. The lecture notes are instantly available to be printed out for personal reference, or to be edited on the screen and adapted for use in a talk given to another group.

Huge Bible resources on the Net

For some years programs have been available to provide concordances on disks, sometimes with more than one version of the Bible displayed side by side on the screen. Many people have found this invaluable, especially as the result can be an instantly printed neat list of typed verses suitable for an overhead acetate.

However, almost every facility in these programs (which are costly) is now available free on the Net, not just in English but in many other languages too. What is more, the speed is impressive, even with complicated searches, typically locating thirty or forty correct verses in around four seconds. Ordinary concordances only allow a search on a single word. Computer concordances allow you to type in any cluster of words or phrases you like.

There is already a host of Bible study resources on the Net, far more powerful than anything you can currently buy in the shops. For example, many Christians find a concordance invaluable, where a word or phrase can be looked up in a large volume, and the verse it comes from identified. Ideas can easily be tracked from the first verse of Genesis to the last verse of Revelation by reading the entire list of passages containing particular words. This is an extremely useful tool in preparing teaching on various subjects, while taking care to avoid the serious pitfalls of quoting verses out of their proper context.

Concordances and Bible dictionaries

Here are three that I tried using Bible Gateway (http://www.gospelcom.Net/Bible):

'Bravest warriors' produced Amos 2:16 – 'Even the bravest warriors will flee naked on that day' – in four seconds.

'One another' produced a list of 224 verses in five seconds.

'Cart crushes grain' produced Amos 2:13 – 'I will crush you as a cart crushes when loaded with grain' – in four seconds.

Of course, if you simply want to check a single verse, a printed concordance wins easily on time because of the hassle of turning on the computer and going online in the first place. But extended research is far better suited to electronic data, and the Internet is both fast and free.

There are free Bible dictionaries on the Net, such as the Easton's Bible Dictionary. Then there are Nave's Topical Bible, Scripture Studies, Matthew Henry's Concise Commentary on the Whole Bible and the World Wide Study Bible, to name just a few. If you are interested in manuscripts, you might like to try the Electronic New Testament Manuscripts Project, or to look at the Dead Sea Scrolls. Every denominational resource you could think of is on the Net, including the Book of Common Prayer.

Powerful tool for researching

The Internet is quite simply the largest, most powerful and fastest library you could possibly find – as well as the fastest growing. Where else can you locate 50 million documents so easily? My first port of call when researching just about any subject now is the Net, unless there is a familiar book in my large personal library which I know is likely to contain the information.

A few hours ago I had a call from a professional actress, a Christian, who has just received a commission to write a short play. She had a query about a story on genetically engineered food that had been in the press earlier in the week, and wanted more information. I said I would phone her back, and in less than ten minutes I had logged onto the Net and found several relevant pages, including two newsgroup contributions and an official company report. It was everything she needed. I printed out the pages and faxed them, but if she had been on e-mail, the answers would have been on her own screen a couple of minutes later.

Fresh discoveries are just around the corner

One strength of the Net is that it encourages you to explore. The hyperlink system means that even having identified the three facts you may have been searching for, it takes just a second or two more to trigger a wonderful cascade of new information, perhaps from other sites thousands of miles away, yet directly related to the same area of interest. All kinds of remarkable discoveries may lie just around the corner, a couple of mouse-clicks away. It is similar to the entertainment value of walking around a well-run large library. There may be many things that catch your eye along the way to finding what you want.

As an undergraduate at Cambridge University I had my own reader's card to the University Library, one of only five copyright libraries in Britain. That library has a copy by law of every single publication – whether a book, magazine, newspaper or booklet – published anywhere in the UK. Unlike the old British Museum library where the public are kept out of the stacks, we were allowed to wander up the metal rung staircases and along literally mile after mile of bookcases. It was all beautifully indexed and laid out so that once you found the book you wanted, you were likely to find a hundred others you had never heard of on exactly the same issues, perhaps going back some 200 years. Every visit there was a fascinating and stimulating experience. The experience of surfing the Internet is similar, clicking on from one idea to another, printing selected pages out as one goes.

In comparison with Cambridge University Library the Net is minuscule, with only the equivalent of 100,000 books online, but with thousands of new pages added every week, and with accelerating growth, one can only guess how much of the world's wisdom will be on the Net in the future. Much of it may be copyright free, either because the copyright has expired, or because the authors are willing to surrender copyrights. Having said that, there is doubtless a great deal of material already on the Net which is there in flagrant breach of copyright. This is another aspect of the difficulty in policing the Net, and represents a serious concern to the publishing industry.

After all, it takes only a few seconds to convert a page of text on paper using a scanner, perhaps an hour for an entire book.

Optical scanners turn books into web-pages

Scanners can be as small as half the size of the book you are reading, and act like photocopiers, except the paper image is produced on the computer screen instead of on another piece of paper. A clever program then reads the patterns of text, and through optical character recognition converts the image into the original keystrokes, just as if you had typed the whole thing in yourself. Once loaded, the text can be edited by word-processors and graphics programs, or indeed by Internet web-site programs.

Converting existing training resources, manuals or recent books to computer data is even easier. Most books written in the last fifteen years have been written on a computer in the first place, or were typeset using one, so the text can be converted directly from one electronic form into another.

While older books may be copyright free, many other more recent works may be out of print and unlikely ever to appear again in a new edition. All these too can be electronically published at almost no cost. Many authors will be delighted to know that their out-of-print works can be obtained once again. This is an important issue now that many publishers remainder their stock after a year or two in the case of poorly selling titles. Once on the Net and using the search engines, automatic indexing means that a considerable number of people may be directed to particular pages of the book as they enter key words or phrases that the author has used.

Summary

Information in. For Christians, and perhaps especially for Christian leaders, the Internet provides massive resources of information we can draw on. There are already numerous online Bibles, study aids, concordances, etc. More broadly, the Net can provide the latest information about current affairs or moral and ethical subjects, such as genetic engineering, so that Christians can speak with the authority that comes from an informed position. The Internet can also provide information that can help with pastoral issues, such as research on bereavement or substance abuse.

Information out. The Internet provides an excellent teaching medium. It can be used simply to allow people who missed a sermon to catch up, or it can be used for discipleship courses and training. Teaching materials can be multimedia, and hyperlinked to other resources to allow students to delve more deeply. Students can be anywhere in the world, or moving from place to place, and they can tailor the speed and content of their studies to suit their needs and circumstances.

CHAPTER 7

Cyberprayer and Cyberworship

The corporate dimension

Prayer and worship are central to the Christian faith. And both fundamentally have a corporate dimension.

Of course we can all pray on our own, and doubtless that is where most prayer occurs. We can also worship on our own, and once again every believer is called to be a worshipper in heart. Nevertheless, there is an extra dimension when the people of God come together for prayer and worship. There is a unique expression of our oneness in Christ, our identity as his body, which flows from these corporate activities.

Millions of believers unite together

I often reflect that every Sunday hundreds of millions of believers unite in a common aim, giving honour to God. They are declaring in the words of Jesus: 'Your kingdom come, your will be done' (Matthew 6:10). Every hour on the hour, throughout the day, as the sun rises and the earth turns, in nation after nation, tens of millions assemble in small to large groups, as a joint expression of the whole community of Christ, his body on earth. There have never been so many followers of Christ alive at one time, and there has never been a time in the history of humanity when so many have found faith each week. While world population growth is running at 1.7% per year, the church is growing at 2.7% per year. So how does cyberchurch worship fit into the picture?

Jesus himself said that when two or three come together

in his name, he is there with them. Unity of purpose is the key. 'If two of you on earth agree about anything you ask for, it will be done for you by my Father in heaven' (Matthew 18:19–20). However, our information age today allows two people to agree at the same moment to pray together about the same thing, yet be separated by long distances.

I cannot recall how many times someone has telephoned me about an issue and after discussing it, we have agreed to pray together there and then, either while still connected or immediately on hanging up. There is hardly any difference between this and an Internet Relay Chat prayer communication taking place live.

Praying together works

It would be dangerously simplistic to say that the more people who pray, the more effective it is. Nevertheless, the Scriptures, both Old Testament and New, are full of instances where the people of God assemble together to pray. The writer to the Hebrews exhorts his readers not to neglect meeting together, and we know from Acts 2:42 that prayer was a central component in the gatherings of the first-century church

God's power is released as people pray together. At many points of crisis in both Old and New Testaments we are told that deliverance came out of a time of assembled prayer and worship. For example, the disciples pray together in Acts 1 and 2 before the coming of the Holy Spirit, and again in Acts 4:31. Other examples are the crying out to God by the Israelites in Exodus 2:23, prayer and worship of the people with Moses in Exodus 4:31, the coming down of God's glory as the Israelites worship God in the wilderness, national thanksgiving in Joshua 5:10, marching round Jericho in Joshua 6, the assembly of the people by Samuel at Mizpah and later at Gilgal (1 Samuel 10 and 11) and so on.

The example of Jesus

The Psalms make no sense at all except in the context of corporate worship. Jesus and his earliest followers taught by example that it was utterly unthinkable for a man or woman of God to exist in isolation – except for a limited period when called by God for a specific reason to withdraw from all social contact, as Jesus did himself for forty days in the wilderness.

We might conclude then that while the Internet can fulfil the condition of two or three agreeing together in prayer, it is unlikely to fulfil the conditions for an assembly. But are we being too rigid here? If Jesus is present with two believers talking to each other and praying on the telephone, and therefore in the midst of an Internet voice call or video link for similar purposes, and also in an Internet Relay Chat prayer link, then what is the situation with a larger electronic gathering?

Large electronic prayer gatherings

Does such electronic prayer have greater impact if three or four people are using the telephone together, all listening in on extensions or using standard conference call facilities? Is Internet Relay prayer more effective when twenty or thirty people are being led in prayer simultaneously in different parts of the world, with each participant able to contribute a prayer of their own or a scripture or some word of encouragement?

We may conclude then that any form of live human interaction – even at a distance – if an expression of prayer and worship, is likely to have a particular spiritual significance. It may be that the degree of significance depends on the degree of involvement of the participants; the intensity of their oneness as they express their united hearts and minds to God. There are many mysteries here.

And surely many possibilities. After all, we are familiar

with the idea of a prayer letter, which may be local, national or international in scope. Often the prayer requests are necessarily of a very general nature, otherwise they would be out of date by the time they were circulated. But using the Internet, a prayer letter can be updated as events unfold and this would allow prayers to be far more specific and better targeted. People praying this way would also have much quicker feedback on answered prayers, which would be very good for motivation. We are not far away from the exciting possibility of global networking in a time of crisis – say, mobilising a million e-mail protesters in three days, writing to embassies about a sudden death sentence imposed on a Christian leader and his family.

Electronic worship is not so strange

Turning from prayer to worship, we find some of the same parallels. For example, it is very common for Christians to enjoy listening to worship tapes in the car. Is Jesus any less present if the driver is alone than when the driver is a part of a congregation worshipping?

Many Christians would attest to the extraordinary way in which God has met them personally while listening to a tape of people worshipping God. This can be especially true if the tape is of a meeting at the church where the person usually attends. Christian radio stations also thrive on the fact that listening live to worship can be very helpful to people in their own devotional life, wherever they may be.

A more immediate form of this is an intercom relay of a church service to a crèche area or an overflow room. There are few people who would deny that listening like this is a valid way of taking part, although most would probably agree that it is much harder to feel involved in what is happening; that they are missing out on some dimensions of what is happening in the meeting itself. Radio broadcasts are a longer-distance version of the same concept.

Pre-recorded radio transmissions or tapes are a further step along the same path.

In that context, cyberworship may not be so very strange after all, and may not cross any more boundaries than have been crossed years ago using old technology. The person listening to live or pre-recorded worship on his computer using the Net is in exactly the same situation as the person listening to the radio or a tape or television programme, or as someone in the early church listening to a reading of one of the apostle Paul's letters and responding in prayer.

Time-lapse cyberprayer

Time-lapse cyberprayer could be in some measure the same. Many people pray along with prayers recorded on a worship or ministry tape, or during a pre-recorded radio or television broadcast of a church service. This is so similar to what can occur on the Internet using data storage of video and sound files as to be logically indistinguishable.

A time-lapse cyberprayer might be where, for example, someone posts a prayer request to a newsgroup, and thousands of others are prompted to pray as a result over the following weeks. It might also take place where instead of someone reading a written prayer request, they hear a prayer request while connected online, perhaps when listening to a pre-recorded cyberservice.

But the worry is that in future a believer's total experience of church might be confined to these electronic representations. Once again these concerns are nothing new. They are part of the reason why many have had reservations about Christian television channels if they become a substitute for social interaction and lead to a superficial Christianity without any human obligations.

Cyberchurch is no substitute for real-life membership

After all, a fundamental command from Jesus to his disciples was that they must love each other. He told them that their love for each other would be a sign of the kingdom, an unmistakable demonstration that they were his followers (John 13:34–35). But love requires involvement. Jesus was not talking of sentimental love but of family *agape* love. To all who believed on his name, he gave the right to become children of God (John 1:12).

We are brothers and sisters to each other, in close relationship, with eternal bonds of mutual commitment and self-sacrifice. The biblical picture of a church is of a gathered community, a royal priesthood, a holy nation, a people called by God out of darkness into his marvellous light (1 Peter 2:9). None of this can be fulfilled merely by virtual reality friendships, where people can unplug the modem every time they feel like giving up on people.

Interactive cyberpreaching will be possible

The technology will no doubt allow us to move from Internet broadcasts or playback of recordings to true interactivity on a large scale. In the future it might be possible to see a composite image of an electronic congregation of fifty or a hundred faces on your screen, refreshed every minute or two. Each participant's camera image could be sent live to a central computer on the Net, which builds up the total view of the congregation before transmitting it to every participant. The screen might be one of those prehistoric, old-fashioned television monitors sitting as a heavy big box on your desk, or a huge flat panel hung like a picture on the wall.

A cyberpreacher could take his cue from the expressions on their faces, from restlessness or a stifled yawn – signals any preacher reads in the flesh today. A preacher could also allow an individual to pose a question or make a contribution, and allow a close up picture to be sent to everyone as the person replies. Such a cyberservice would have no parallel in recent human experience in the church, although many similar experiments have been carried out by those in other walks of life.

Large-scale video conferences are nothing new

For example, at the medical school where I trained they have been experimenting with large-scale interactive video conferences for years. Charing Cross Hospital in London is a highly specialised medical centre which focuses on care of those suffering from all the rarest and most exotic conditions, and has few patients with common conditions for students to see. So students are scattered into a number of other general hospitals in London.

Travel times are long between these centres and it is extremely inefficient to have lecturers repeat the same topics more than once to different members of the same year group. Their solution was to wire up two or three different lecture theatres so that the main group at the Cross could be joined by the other groups in other remote lecture theatres. To help these students feel more involved, cameras were set up allowing the lecturer to ask questions to different groups and see students replying.

The boredom threshold

But it is hard to feel as personally involved in an electronic experience. Video conferencing rarely has the same impact as personal presence at an important meeting. Television itself condenses down the personality and presence of any speaker. Although some people seem larger than life on the screen compared to when you meet them face to face, usually it is the other way round, hence the need for projection of an appropriate intensity, which is a basic part of any media training.

Concentration span is far less for a television play than for a play in a theatre. It is far easier to get up and go out to make a cup of coffee. There is less of a personal commitment to what is going on. Channel zapping is a universal habit of television watchers and Internet users. A moment of boredom is all it may take for a person to disappear from the audience and wander elsewhere.

One of the real weaknesses of future large-scale cyberchurch meetings was demonstrated in a highly embarrassing incident. There was a lecturer who was well known for being a boring speaker, but the subject was important and attendance was good at every site. From time to time the lecturer would flick a switch to change the screen image in the main auditorium from one of the remote sites to another.

After the lecture had been going for about half an hour he announced that he would now be asking a question of the group at hospital X. To his utter dismay, when he brought the camera image up onto the screen the entire lecture room was empty. Unknown to him, one by one every single medical student had left.

Attention spans as short as twenty seconds

Prime-time television news is usually edited on the basis that the maximum length of time a viewer can cope with is twenty seconds for an edited clip of someone speaking. It is quite surprising to see the difference between how long an item feels and how long it actually is.

Over the years I have done a lot of news interviews on a wide variety of current issues. Almost invariably people I know come up to me and complain: 'They cut you short,' or, 'I was just yelling to my friend to come quickly and it was all over. I had no idea even what you were talking about because it all happened so fast.' I then tell them to get out a stop watch and time how long President Clinton or John Major had on the same bulletin. These important people are doing well to get forty seconds.

Newsmakers reckon that every couple of seconds over the twenty-second limit they lose another chunk of their audience, zapping away to other channels. Apart from the video recorder, the remote control unit has probably done more to alter television viewing habits than anything else over the last fifteen years. No wonder adverts have to be entertaining, with less than twenty seconds to hold people before their featured products are literally wiped off the screens of millions. That is why making commercials is one of the most expensive forms of production in terms of costs per minute of final film.

In comparison, the attention span for radio is far longer, several minutes perhaps. This is partly because of where people listen to it, and the fact that most people are doing something else at the same time. A sound and vision Internet programme is therefore going to need to fight very hard to keep people interested for more than a few seconds. At present, web-page designers face a dilemma: they know that to retain the viewers' attention pages need to be bright, and well illustrated with good quality graphics, and perhaps sound too. However, image and sound files can often be very large indeed and the time taken for them to download can well exceed the frustrated viewer's patience.

Summary

We have seen that worship or prayer on the Internet is in some ways a far less radical step than we might first have thought. It has to be seen in the context of worship and ministry tapes, sound relays, local radio broadcasts, television programmes and telephone calls. However, the Net has huge potential to take Christian practice and experience into new areas – ones perhaps never considered before because the possibilities would have been thought of as pure science fiction. We should see these possibilities as an addition to existing options for worship and fellowship, not as a substitute. Meeting together for worship and to express our love for each other is both a biblical command and a human experience that cannot be replicated electronically.

SECTION 3

Facing the Issues

CHAPTER 8

Cyberaddiction

An issue already

With one in five men in at least one US city spending more than forty hours a week on the Net, many young people have become so hooked into cyberreality that Internet experts are already expressing concerns about cyberaddiction. Could a whole generation become incapable of existing in the normal world without distress?

We first need to understand the psychological mechanisms which draw people to the Net; why it is that the Net can provide a minority of people with a pleasurable alternative to non-cyberlife. Then we can look at what can be done to protect the vulnerable and help the trapped.

Computer addicts have a long history

Fears of addiction to computers are nothing new. From the very first days of video arcade games there were alarm bells about a few children and teenagers who were spending vast sums of money – even stealing – to pay for an arcade habit. Before that time, arcade problems were usually associated with gambling rather than with computer overdosing. Perhaps in a way the earliest games also had a gambling element. There was no payback as such, no cash prize to be won, but a definite reward in terms of the highest scores which were displayed for all to see. Many conventional gambling machines such as one-arm bandits also provide no cash reward, only giving out tokens for further play.

Gambling is often but not always highly addictive. There is some evidence that addictive patterns of behaviour may be associated with particular gene types. This is not to say that genes make us addicts, but the presence of certain genes may make it more likely that someone becomes heavily involved. Genes influence so much of what we are and how we behave – far more than we like to think. (See my book *The Genetic Revolution* for a fuller discussion of this area.)

Computer crazes come and go

The history of video arcade games is a long story of fads and fashions as crazes come and go, and as different generations of children grow up. The first arcade games were quite primitive and soon moved into the living room, displaced by ever more complex computer chips promising more exciting graphics, more realistic special effects.

The biggest growth area was in simulations of aircraft, cars, motorbike races and combat attacks. A revolution also swept through the electronic games section of toy shops. The highest accolade for any system you could buy was that it was almost as good as the systems in the arcades.

An example was the Gameboy, a small hand-held device, capable of playing highly complex games. Millions were sold worldwide in just a couple of years. Hundreds of millions of hours were spent staring at the tiny screens, battling against the odds with fingers and thumbs. When they first came out, it was not unusual for children to spend more than ten hours a week playing on them.

There was another game device that worked by reading bar codes. Any bar codes would do. The play device converted the bar code into numbers, and particular (unknown) numbers triggered an enormous number of bonus points. In Japan children quickly learned by trial and error that particular tins and other food products had bumper scores. The news spread like wildfire through schools and colleges – so much so that there was a shortage of particular items in some shops.

Predictions of disaster unfulfilled

However, the worst predictions of widespread damage to a generation of young people raised on computer games have yet to be realised. Boys more than girls are the heaviest users, but there has been little evidence to suggest that many have been damaged by the experience. There is far more evidence that television, video and films have had a negative impact through promoting violence and indiscriminate sexual activity as normal.

In my view games which simply involve eye/hand co-ordination and fast reaction speeds are unlikely to be damaging. This may be different from some of the latest games which contain explicit violent or pornographic images. One game that has caused great controversy is *Doom*, because of the bloody corpses left on the ground after a shoot-out, because of the life-like indiscriminate massacres of other human beings with guns, rockets and even chain saws, and because the virtual reality format helps create a world of total involvement. However, the most important feature of the game is the 'play factor'. It is extremely well thought out and the graphics are superb – a technological breakthrough when it first came out.

Doom set new levels for realism – and controversy

Doom set the standards for a new level of realism, and in so doing triggered immediate calls for censorship. The game is now age-rated in Britain but not in many other nations, and millions of early copies exist on home computers already. It is probably one of the most widely played games today. A further extension has been to use the Internet to connect several players together who are either working in competition to reach the end first, killing everything in sight on the way, or against each other with direct player-against-player shoot-outs, resulting in player 'death'.

In fact the game sounds far worse on paper than it is in reality. To an adult the images are probably far less disturbing than many scenes in a 15-rated film, and are less emotionally traumatic than many scenes in a 12-rated film. Nevertheless, it is a very violent game which can scare younger players, and it can be highly involving. It is hard to estimate what the effect might be on someone who might have psychopathic tendencies and who has access to firearms. The answer is probably less than the effect of extremely violent and explicit adult-rated films and videos, because the graphics are far less convincing.

As a result of *Doom* and other games, steps have now been taken to provide age-ratings on all games in some countries, including the UK, recognising that the gap between video and video games has narrowed to the point where both need to be considered in a very similar way.

Do computer games make children isolated?

Some people feared that overindulgence in computer games would cause children to become isolated as they stopped talking to each other. However, many computer games are played socially, with one or two watching another play and taking it in turns, and other games allow more than one user to compete simultaneously.

Our own children have gone through intense periods of game playing, but often together, learning from each other the tricks needed to succeed. Each game loses its interest after a while, but the best are resurrected when friends come round to play. One has to consider what the nation's children would be most likely to be doing if not playing computer games. Probably the majority would be sitting at home watching television.

Many computer games provide training for life

Those having fun on computers are acquiring valuable skills from an early age. At least one military training school uses computer games to help speed up pilots' reactions. After all, the action of 'shoot 'em up' games is not so far removed from the skills needed to fly the latest computer controlled combat planes, with headgear displays, electronic targeting and on-screen data to be processed at very high speeds.

Many computer games are highly complex electronic puzzles. There are often very few instructions on new machines in arcades and not many more on computer games that are bought. Children and teenagers become extremely expert through trial and error, and will usually succeed against highly intelligent adults by a process of computer induced intuition, leaps of logic and sheer audacity in trying the unexpected and unlikely. These games stimulate creative thinking, memory and strategic planning.

SimCity – modelling the economy

For example, our latest computer came loaded with a game called *SimCity*, which allows people to create and run their own cities. You start with a large area of wilderness or farmland and build roads, railways, power stations, water supplies and other basic amenities. As you do so, people start arriving, building their own homes, offices, factories and leisure areas.

The art of the game is to raise money through taxation and to spend the municipal budget wisely so that a huge city develops with a reasonable quality of life. For example, if there is too much pollution, people move out and tax revenue falls. It is an excellent economic model, which is absorbing for adults and yet can be played by our seven-year-old son. He has already mastered the art of raising revenue for building road bridges and power stations by increasing taxes or issuing bonds. He knows from experience that cities are really successful when there is the right balance between open space, jobs in factories and offices, homes, and most important of all, road, rail and air communications.

There are many interactive Internet areas designed especially with children in mind of similar educational value where they can, for example, research volcanoes, invent virtual machines and roam the solar system.

Finding hidden keys

Some games can only be completed by discovering features which are hidden. These features are only revealed by pressing a strange combination of keystrokes at particular points. It can take several years before all the secrets of a newly released game are discovered. Many of these undocumented features were created by the programmers for their own use and enjoyment, and were simply never deleted after the game went into production.

However, exactly the same kinds of skills are vital to using 'serious' computer systems, such as spreadsheets, word-processors, desk-top publishing programs and databases. Despite all the progress in technology, many manufacturers are still selling products with faults or bugs. Indeed, most computer systems now sold are so complicated that they are beyond the understanding of any single human brain on earth. An expert may understand most of the program functions, but little of the code and only some of the hardware. A case in point is *Windows 95*, the standard platform on which most things are supposed to run (many programs don't without hours of attention).

Why children are good at solving adult problems

The conflicts between different programs are legion, baffling and very time consuming to sort out. Children raised on computer games are good at solving these problems.

I was first involved myself in microcomputer development and software design in 1978. In my time I have installed systems in several countries and provided computer consultancy for many organisations. Recently I bought one of the most powerful desk-top models available, with an enormous number of different programs. In addition I bought several more, together with a number of add-on devices such as a camera, and attempted to transfer many programs I had used on a small portable, using an earlier version of *Windows*.

Despite excellent telephone support from various suppliers, the problems that emerged were so complex that some were still unresolved several months later – no one was quite sure what was causing the problems. *Windows 95* was supposed to be a well-tested, robust program, with millions of user hours on thousands of systems all over the world before it was even launched, yet *Windows 95* crashes several times a day when I am working the system hard.

I have now sorted out most of the problems by using exactly the same mental processes as in playing many of these computer games: exploring, probing, testing, looking for the hidden and non-obvious.

Computer children will dominate tomorrow's world

I am convinced that a generation brought up on computer games will end up dominating our computer centred world in the years to come. It is already happening. Genius inventors like Sir Clive Sinclair made tens of thousands of ultra-low-cost microcomputers. As a result a very large number of British households with children owned some kind of 'micro' by the early 1980s – one of the highest proportions of any country in the world. Almost all of these multi-purpose boxes were primarily, if not exclusively, used for games.

Ten years later the UK is still one of the world's leading nations when it comes to microcomputer home ownership, with ultra-powerful multimedia PCs leading the way. Home PCs 'for the children' are often faster and more powerful in every way than the computers used by their parents at work. One of the main motivations for buying them has been to help launch their children into a computer dominated world.

So we see that addiction may be a threat but is less of a reality. Internet use is just another kind of computer activity, not dissimilar to what we have seen before. Admittedly there are other worries. Interactive role games have aroused concern among parents because they allow people to create completely new identities for themselves which can be lived out for long periods. They can also be highly realistic and as damaging as some films on videos. However, the longer-term effects of using these programs have also probably been overrated, and over-use is relatively easy to prevent through limiting what programs are permanently installed on the system, monitoring use of CD-ROMs and by limiting game use to certain periods each day.

Some people's lives are being wrecked

Nevertheless, some people's lives are being damaged by computer activity, games and Internet wandering. I am thinking particularly here of adults, who often have far greater access under situations of less supervision than their teenage children. Internet involvement can affect partners and children.

The term 'computer widow' has become increasingly common, describing a pattern where the husband remains glued to his computer screen at home until the early hours of the morning, apparently oblivious to the time, while his wife frets away, fighting her growing sense of isolation and loneliness, or pouring emotional and mental energy into activities of her own.

One key element of the Internet – indeed of many other computer systems – is that the user loses all sense of time, and becomes locked into highly intense concentration. We saw earlier how television news has difficulty keeping someone's attention for more than a few seconds, yet a computer application could keep the same person fixed to the keyboard and screen for eight hours or more without more than a couple of five-minute breaks.

How to detect a cyberaddict

The key to the diagnosis of cyberaddiction is whether there are untoward effects on other areas of people's lives. Here are some questions to help you to decide whether a pattern of use is healthy or not:

- How many hours a week are spent on this activity?
- Before the Internet arrived, how would that time have been used, i.e. is it just replacing television soaps and comedy programmes?
- Is the intensity of involvement a significant factor to others, as well as the time involved, e.g. do people find it hard to drift into the room and say 'hello'?
- Is the person becoming reclusive for long periods?
- Can this habit be afforded? How much money is being spent on the Internet each month, including phone, access time and other equipment, programs or books purchased to improve the service?
- Has there been proper discussion about this?
- Are key relationships being neglected?
- Is work suffering, either because the person is accessing pages on the Net during work hours that are nothing to do with work, or because the person has been 'moon-lighting' on the Net and is tired the following day?
- Most important of all, what is the effect if the person is not able to access the Internet for a day, a week, a month?

Primary and secondary Internet addiction

Some people clearly are addicted in the sense that they are losing control, spending more money than they should, neglecting other commitments and showing signs of irritability and restlessness if not connected. For them, cyberspace is an obsession. Primary Internet addiction is a mental state of dependency induced by over-exposure to the Internet medium. Secondary Internet addiction is a mental state of dependency induced by over-exposure to an Internet message, for example Internet pornography. The latter is not a true Internet addiction, since the real problem lies in another area of life which is not confined to the Net.

Another motivation for Internet involvement can be to say 'hello' to cyberfriends rather than just trying out new web-sites. The equivalent of this is meeting every night for a drink in the local pub or wine bar. There may be a group of friends who enjoy meeting up every day. There may be some kind of obligation to show up. Internet Relay Chat can be like that.

In conclusion, then, all computer systems have a great potential to be mentally absorbing to the point where other activities may be forced to take second place. Many users would admit to losing track of the time, to being shocked at how long they have been at the desk, but although addiction can result, it is by no means inevitable.

How to treat Internet addiction

Here are some steps to take to help those with cyber-addiction.

1. Get them to recognise the problem. The first step with any kind of addiction is to help the person recognise that there is a problem. The Internet user may not be aware of this until confronted by neglect of primary responsibilities, or the phone bill, or Internet withdrawal, say, while on holiday.

2. Wait for them to ask for help. The second step is for the user to be willing to ask for help. Part of this is being willing to submit to the help when it is given. This allows another person to be supportive and directional about agreeing together and helping implement some ground rules.

3. Rationing. The third step is to place some limits on the Internet use. There are a number of programs available, directed mainly at children and adolescents, but which are capable of being used by anyone. These allow a person to enter a password protected area where different Internet access accounts can be created, fixing a limit on the number of hours' use by each person. If the person who has the password is a non-enthusiast – say the wife of an addicted husband – then that will impose some constraint. The wife could also have the password to set blocks on certain types of site – pornography for example – in cases of secondary addiction. This may be considered by most to be a far less satisfactory option than the simple measure of self-control, but it all depends on the degree of addiction.

4. Supervision. Rationing and supervision go together. Another step might be to move the location of the computer out of a spare bedroom into a reception room in the main part of the house. This would allow a greater interaction with those using the computer.

5. Disposal. A final option if all else fails is disposal of the system altogether. There is life after the Internet. Throwing away the modem and cancelling the account may be helpful and might even save a marriage. However, there are growing numbers of people who have to use the Internet for work, so total Internet isolation may be impractical.

Summary

Concern about the impact of the Internet on children might be overstated. Computers and the Internet provide a much more interactive, participative environment than passively watching television. The Internet can be a great educational tool, precisely because children find it so engaging. The risk of social isolation is tempered by the fact that children often play on computers together. In any case, children have always had a capacity to become highly absorbed in solitary activities that they enjoy, such as model-making or reading comics for hours on end. Computer games can be useful at developing hand/eye co-ordination, and teaching problem-solving skills.

There are dangers from extremely violent games (see next chapter), and computer and Internet addiction does exist, both in children and adults. As with all addictions, this can be highly destructive to relationships. Christians need to be conscious of this danger, and church ministers need to be alert to this risk to members of their congregations.

CHAPTER 9

Cybercensorship

Mind pollution?

The Net is a composite of everything that is good and everything that is bad in publishing, radio and television, as well as the murkier side of the video industry. Anarchists, bomb-makers, drug dealers, paedophiles and sellers of obscene materials can all operate almost without fear of control in the cyberworld. More than a million children are estimated to be Net users, raising fears of exposure to all kinds of undesirable influences.

Since the Net is becoming so secure, it is hardly surprising that it has acted as a magnet for people who have something to hide. And since the Internet search engines are so powerful, it takes just a few seconds to locate the one person in a million with a particular rare (and possibly dangerous) obsession or interest.

For example, there is a fairly continuous stream of information on bomb-making which is easy to access – just type 'bomb-making'. A few months ago I was surprised to find detailed instructions on making a home-made grenade. More recently there was a request from a student for instructions on how to make a bomb from fertiliser. The bomb attack in Oklahoma was said to have been aided possibly by bomb-making information on the Net. A couple of weeks after the bombing, two teen-agers in New York were injured making a pipe bomb. One Internet listing for pipe bomb instructions was still visible as late as September 1996, although the web-site link had been disabled.

Human beings have never had so much power to link so

rapidly with others of like mind. In ancient societies one's social circle was limited to a village, town or tribe. Even tentatively expressing an eccentric wish or deviant thought would have been to risk ostracisation or worse. But today the darkest of dark thoughts can be revealed anonymously in cyberspace, with pointers for people of like mind to get in touch via e-mail. However, such people are taking risks that other people attracted to their e-mail boxes may be looking to gain evidence leading to a prosecution.

Also of concern from a Christian point of view, the Internet is an ideal medium for the cults, since it enables them to promulgate their views and recruit widely at very low cost.

Internet more powerful than the CIA or FBI

So how do you control a system created by some of the best military minds in the world with the express purpose of making it impossible to control? Let us take the example of someone distributing obscene pictures. Remember that the person may be doing this for free, as part of the culture of the Internet. If the person is in a country where there are strict controls, the Internet provider may come under pressure to cut his links. However, by the time that happens, a hundred other individuals elsewhere in the world may have downloaded the whole file and put it up in their own web-space.

Heavily advertised sites are easy for authorities to find, but private sites are not. Encryption makes it far more difficult still. Military-grade scrambling of all electronic communications is an option for everyone who has a modem. Various large computers in different countries spend all their time exploring web-pages and indexing them. There is no reason why a similar system could not be set up to monitor for unsavoury sites, but decoding would be almost impossible.

Is the carrier responsible for content? Is a telecom company responsible for a person's verbal abuse of another person down a copper wire? Is a mobile phone company responsible if a telephone is used to carry out a crime or to evade capture by the police? Is a newsagent responsible for the libel in a newspaper? Is an Internet provider responsible for the quality of all data whizzing down its lines? How can any provider hope to monitor the vast volumes of traffic?

Controls can work – in part

Controls can and do work, but they are not absolutely effective. The first level to consider is international agreements. Unfortunately this is hardly likely to be practical, as we have seen over satellite television. For example, China has been unable to persuade foreign-owned multimedia companies not to broadcast 'subversive' entertainment programmes into their country. As a result some 40 million Chinese citizens are able to watch material banned by a strong dictatorship.

Another example is the case of Britain, swamped by satellite channels from Europe, many of which have very different standards from those for British terrestrial television. Having said this, there are moves already among major Internet providers to provide standards which may eventually form the basis of informal international agreements.

National codes of practice

The next level to consider is national codes of practice. These appear to be more workable at first sight but are also fraught with difficulties. In Germany recently steps were taken to ban certain subversive newsgroups and bulletin boards. Because the service provider involved did not have the ability to close down access to parts of their global system in one country only, for a time all this provider's clients across the world were denied access to these offending sites just because of action within one country. The technical problems were soon overcome, however, and the provider restored control-free access for its customers in the rest of the world. So, although preventive action was difficult, it did show the power of concerted action by a few individuals.

China has attempted to impose national controls, as has Singapore, by insisting that all Internet traffic is routed via government owned computer systems, allowing electronic scanning and human monitoring. China's attempts have been weakened by the proximity of Hong Kong. Internet users in mainland China only have to dial into a computer in Hong Kong that is linked to the Net, and every control is broken.

The Singapore censorship began in September 1996, with a block on any of 100,000 Internet users using the Net without doing so via a government server. Each page request is checked against a known list of unsuitable sites. If the site is banned, the message 'Not suitable' appears. Singapore has classified the Net as a broadcast medium, so it falls under the remit of existing legislation. Once again it will be hard to stop someone calling an Internet provider outside the country, and impossible to stop direct dialling of one computer system by another (bulletin boards), not using the Net.

In contrast, the UK Internet comes under the remit of the Metropolitan Police's Clubs and Vice Unit. A letter was sent recently by them to all Internet service providers in Britain with a veiled threat of government action if they did not sort out the pornography problem themselves. They may try using a standard filtering service. For example, the new Safety Net Foundation is aiming to filter out 99.9% of child pornography and other offending sites using similar screening mechanisms on a voluntary basis, offered to other Internet providers to help clean up their information flow. A key element in keeping indexes up to date may be a continuous flow of information from members of the public about sites they would like to see restricted.

Big Brother is watching you

New technology does give dictatorships immense new powers to monitor citizens, and it is not inconceivable that the current information free-for-all will be replaced one day by quite severe authoritarian information controls in many parts of the world.

It is sobering to realise that no new technology would be required to link tens of thousands of video spy cameras into the Net with a special password allowing intelligence services to watch what is going on in every room inside the homes of political dissidents. The watchers could be sitting at a computer terminal anywhere in the world.

A click with a mouse would be all that was needed to switch from one home to another, or from a living room to a bedroom, constantly following people around, perhaps listening in too, with severe fines if any camera or microphone is found to have been interfered with. The cost of wiring up an entire home like this would probably be less than £5,000 plus the costs of a dedicated phone line. This is cheaper than conventional surveillance which uses watchers outside a house or secret bugging devices attached to radio transmitters.

Simple devices are already available to read car number plates on traffic cameras. These are said to be 85% accurate in good conditions. If these were also linked to the Net it would mean any authorised person located anywhere in the world could track the location and movements of any vehicle in an entire nation, or even in other nations.

Policing of e-mail and web-sites

In the same way, imaginative use of technology will allow all kinds of web-site and e-mail activity to be monitored, leading to the arrest of people suspected of criminality. While encryption programs will mean intelligence services may not be aware of the content of transmissions, the fact that very large amounts of encrypted information are being sent from one private individual to other private individuals should be enough to alert suspicion and prompt a preliminary investigation. An electronic trail can be followed, since the one thing that cannot be encoded is the e-mail address, signalling the next destination in a distribution process.

Simple measures to make Internet policing easier could include a new rule insisting that all computer systems and users reveal their identities every time they access a page of information, so that access trails can be logged. In practice many Internet users may be surprised to know that their details are already flashed around the world. Internet providers vary in the level of anonymity they provide.

Some people have been so worried about the 'Big Brother' monitoring of activity online that they have started using anonymous web-servers. You call the anonymiser web-site, which then carries out all your requests for pages, sending the data on to you while withholding information about who you are.

These battles will continue to rage, and I expect the upper hand will be gained by regulation. But voluntary regulation is unlikely to be complete. It may eliminate the worst, but a great amount of unsavoury material is still likely to get through.

So we can see that whenever we talk about controls, there are arguments in favour (elimination of corrupting and criminal influences) and arguments against (individual and religious freedoms which once compromised may be removed completely by an oppressive regime).

Age controls on adult sites

In the US several new trends have emerged as a counter-attack on the pornographic Internet industry. First, some major Internet providers are now making an advertising feature out of the fact that they regulate the quality of sites available. Secondly, organisations like Microsoft have built into their programs new screening devices which look for an age classification on web-pages (where websites have bothered to use them). Thirdly, a US clampdown has encouraged many adult sites to prove that viewers are over eighteen. Without a special password – standard issue from a common registration area – access is blocked. But we must ask how easy it is for a child to masquerade as an adult to get an adult site pass.

Despite rapid changes to the way many US adult sites are running, there is still a massive gap because sites in most other nations are not covered at all, and it takes only a few hours to move the contents of an entire site from one country to another, leaving just a short notice plus a hyperlink at the original location.

So long as demand is there, someone will supply

Unfortunately, cybersex is a money spinner and is no more likely to be pushed out of the Internet than prostitutes off the streets. Every aspect of the new technology is being used to deliver, including two-way video conferencing, as well as text and photographs. A lot of this is not commercialised, but just people experimenting with what the Internet can do.

And once the data is on a local computer it can also be distributed to friends on ordinary floppy disks, or e-mailed instantly around the world, the office, the college or the school. With e-mail an Internet user can push one button to send a large file automatically to several thousands of people, in a process taking a couple of minutes and costing almost nothing.

Most effective controls are home-based

So, then, we have seen that there are steps which can be taken in law or by consensus, at national and international levels. However, the most effective controls of all may be at the level of the local user. One method is to use a special program such as *Cyber-Sitter* installed in your own computer. There are several such programs and they all work in a similar way.

First, *Cyber-Sitter* has a list of more than 5,000 objectionable sites. Access to these is blocked. Because thousands of new sites appear on the Internet every week, free update lists can be downloaded at any time. *Cyber-Sitter* relies on current users to inform them of new sites to avoid.

Secondly, the program scans all text for suspicious words. If any of these appear, the site is blocked or the words are deleted. The results can sometimes be bizarre, because so many words now have double meanings.

Thirdly, users can opt to ban downloads of images in special formats favoured by adult site providers. The program is password protected and can be hidden so that it does not appear in any directory. The user is completely unaware of its operation. Blocking of banned sites is cleverly disguised. When an attempt to gain access is made, one of a number of very common Internet error messages is flashed up on the screen, giving the impression that the Net itself has developed a fault, such as not being able to locate the proper address of the site.

Who sets the standards?

Of course, as with any method of censorship, the biggest issue of all is who decides where the fine line falls between the acceptable and the non-acceptable. Parents differ when it comes to what they allow their children to watch on television, and would doubtless do so if they were asked to reach a consensus over certain Net sites. In other words, *Cyber-Sitter* and other such programs work on trust, on the basis that the users believe in the sound judgement of the people who decide which sites are blocked and which are not.

Logging of activity is important

An important option is the automatic logging of every visit or attempted visit to a site, and a record of any violations. The controls can also be set to prevent access to bulletin boards (direct dialling of other computers not on the Net). Many of these are just other PC users with a modem and files on a hard disk which can be copied, all linked to a premium rate telephone line.

A practical solution at home

My favoured option is an up-to-date version of a program like *Cyber-Sitter*, possibly combined with an Internet provider with a 'family' policy, and some kind of adult monitoring. One effective but unobtrusive way to provide indirect supervision, and to keep track of what is happening, is for the child to know that every site visited is logged, and to be aware of what the ground rules are.

Unfortunately, whatever controls may exist in your home, there is nothing to stop a child going round to the house of a friend and investigating adult sites there. That is also the situation for videos and satellite viewing. The biggest gap in controls of all can be different standards among other adults in other homes.

There is also nothing to stop distribution of downloaded files by friends at school. It only takes a few seconds to duplicate a disk which could contain thirty or more compressed images. Blank disks cost less than a magazine and they can be copied using any school personal computer, or at home.

Summary

Encourage the best, discourage the worst. The Internet is being used for all kinds of purposes – some good, some neutral and some bad. As with any other medium, we have a responsibility to do all we can to encourage the best and discourage or eliminate the worst. Where our children are concerned, the Internet is just another medium to which they are all increasingly exposed, inside and outside the home.

As with other issues such as smoking, alcohol abuse, taking illegal drugs or sexual activity outside marriage, we need to recognise that the most important factor of all is not access but demand. Oppressive over-supervision is likely to lead only to rebellion, and you cannot be there all the time. One day they will have left home and will need a different kind of supervision – the supervision that comes from their own minds as part of mature decisions they make about themselves and the world they live in.

Therefore, as in any other area of life, supervision best takes place in an environment where issues are openly discussed and debated in the context of a loving, secure home built on Christian values, and where there is a good parental example. As children find faith and guiding values for themselves, they become to an increasing extent their own guardians. They are then less likely to have under-age sex, to abuse drugs or to abuse Internet access.

There is no point putting our heads in the sand and hoping that Internet problems will go away; nor can we just ignore the medium or rage against it all. The Internet is here to stay. Computer networks will be an increasingly important part of our lives and we need to be involved. We cannot expect our children to be lifetime Internet abstainers. There is no reason why they should be.

Freedom from persecution. Finally, we need to remember that any new measures used to track down undesirable groups on the Internet could also be turned against Christians as another means of persecution in states hostile to the gospel.

Christians in countries where churches are persecuted may be deeply grateful for the lack of controls on the Internet. Cyberchurch could be the one area of Christian witness that evades censorship and control, say, in a Muslim country. This is a vitally important role for the Internet to play. We need to remember that censorship can be a double-edged sword.

CHAPTER 10

Cyberthought

Plug in your own brain

The Internet is a psychological event, a new way of thinking, and as we have seen, it can be highly engaging to the
point of addiction. You will need to spend time on the
Internet yourself to appreciate fully the dynamics of this.
When you are on the Internet, you have effectively
plugged your brain into an electronic universe. You are
part of an electronic eye/brain/finger link system that
allows flow of mental activity direct from one human
brain into another. The effect is far more dramatic than
the communication of an idea from an author to a reader in
printed text alone, because of the element of interactivity.
This is a two-way flow of mind and data. You need to
allow your own brain to leap around cyberspace, following its own unique way of thinking. You will find that it
begins to concentrate your mind in an entirely different
way.

Left brain and right brain

The human brain has two hemispheres which operate in
different ways. The left brain is where logical, rational and
verbal thought is centred. It also handles abstract con-
cepts. The right brain is where intuitive, creative and
visual thinking is centred, and where sensory experiences
are processed.

For many people, most of our learning experiences in
the past have been orientated around left-brained thinking:
books and lectures force us to learn in a sequential, logical
way, reading or listening from the beginning to the end.

But part of us is always seeking to involve our right brain much more. Many people have found nonlinear ways to plough through papers and books by skim-reading techniques. They are subconsciously trying to emulate with written words the way in which they watch the world, glancing here and there. I confess I often start reading the end of a book, then I read the beginning and finally dip through the middle, scanning most pages at speed. By the end I can probably give you a fair summary of the main arguments in a fraction of the time of conventional reading.

We see this same process when people go to a good science museum: eyes and feet start wandering all over the place, gathering data, learning about the world, pushing buttons, scanning diagrams, feeling models.

Internet opens the floodgates

The Internet opens the floodgates to right-brained thinking. Of course, much of what we look at on Internet pages is text, and we follow a chain of ideas, both of which appeal to our left brain. But hypertext links open up radical new possibilities, making it possible to read just a few sentences on the text of twenty different pages, switching across from one idea to another, going deeper and deeper through layers of ideas and information until one is satisfied, then instantly rising up again to more general levels, before plunging down deep into detail along another path. There is an intuitive dimension to this, a capacity to make creative leaps of the imagination and to follow them up immediately.

Not only this, the Internet is a multi-dimensional, multimedia world which makes extensive use of images, movement, colour, sound, three-dimensionality and perhaps eventually, as virtual reality develops, even touch. It's a world in which we are participating and initiating, not merely passively responding. By using our left brain and also unleashing the potential of our right brain, communication can take place at incredible speed. It's perhaps not surprising that many people find using the Internet so absorbing.

The fusion of mind and machine

The fusion of mind and machine is deeply satisfying to many personalities, and the resultant absorption is greater than that involved in many other activities. Studies show that intensive computer use for work or leisure is highly stimulating: blood pressure rises releasing hormones, burning up aggression and stimulating the immune system. Of course, prolonged overstimulation can cause problems.

In terms of the depth of prolonged concentration, a parallel can be drawn with the reader of a long novel or thriller, who is inseparable from the book for periods of more than a few minutes, has no interest in being called to meals or to the telephone, or in engaging in any other activity. Even at the meal table the avid reader remains mentally involved in the story, impatient to turn the next page.

A good novel or thriller creates an intensely interesting personal world; a combined product of the writer and the imagination of the reader. The two become one. Thus each person's experience when reading a book is to some extent unique. This is unlike watching a film, where all the mental work is done for you. That is why radio is more absorbing than television; why audio attention span is longer. Radio also engages the imagination of the listener to create the missing images and locations.

Computer/brain fusion leads to prolific activity

The positive side of computer/brain fusion is that computer systems can generate prolific productivity from some types of people, because they keep working at a very intense mental level. That is precisely what is happening as I am writing this book. It has not been unusual for me to sit here typing away or editing on-screen for up to five or more hours with no break at all. One morning the mood caught me and I began early in the day before having any breakfast, intending to have a break after about an hour.

By mid-afternoon I suddenly realised that I had forgotten about breakfast, and lunch had also passed me by in an empty house with no distractions beyond the occasional telephone call. Am I just another computer junky, or an example of someone enjoying computer-assisted high productivity? In those five hours I wrote more than 7,000 words of a first draft (a small paperback is around 40,000). That seems to me to be quite efficient. In the evening I enjoyed a good meal and some time off after a day that felt short but satisfying.

It is true that I could also have written for quite a while using pen and paper, but the concentration span is less, and physical effort more. When you write on a computer, a quick glance back over what you have written often leads straight to editing and expansion, which is not so easy with a handwritten text.

Last night I thought I would kill a spare half hour and look up a small cluster of pages on the Internet for this book, taking advantage of cheap phone rates. I wanted to find some information on newsgroups and print a few out to use as examples. I found some of what I wanted in ten minutes, but along the way my eye kept on being caught by other fascinating things. For example, I saw a reference to photographs of the Dead Sea Scrolls. These ancient fragments are 2,000 years old but were only discovered just a few decades ago. Until very recently access to the Scrolls was strictly limited to a few scholars, despite a big international row. Therefore I was surprised and fascinated to see whole pages of the Scrolls reproduced in colour on my screen, complete with full explanations, indexing and translations. In a few minutes, I had printed out part of the Scrolls to look at later in more detail.

Before I knew it I had spent more than an hour online; it had felt like twenty minutes.

Is that addiction, or just a sign that the Internet is a very effective learning experience? If you think of the difficulties many parents have in persuading their children to get down to serious homework, or to open a large encyclopaedia for pleasure to research a project, then one might welcome such a challenging and interesting global learning tool.

Culture penetration

It seems clear that Internet styles of thinking will progressively penetrate our culture. The CD-ROMs used on computers in most of our schools are already familiarising a new generation with more intuitive right-brained ways of thinking, and this will accelerate as more and more schools become Internet connected. In any case, most tertiary educational establishments have Internet access available to students. If as a society we begin to think in new ways, what are the implications for the church?

Church styles of communication

Current styles of communication within the church largely reflect the cultural history of Europe over the last few centuries. The introduction of printing, followed by rationalism and the Enlightenment, has paved the way for technological developments and modern scientific methodology, and all this has created a culture in which left-brained thinking has predominated. It is only now that this is being seriously challenged. The church mirrored these cultural trends, moving away from the right-brained means of communication used in the Middle Ages, such as stained glass, icons, cathedral architecture, mystery plays, ceremonials, festivals, etc. towards more left-brained forms: reading the Bible, the analytical sermon. Both printing and listening to sermons are unidirectional, and learning is much more in danger of becoming a passive exercise.

A new challenge

As Internet-style thinking becomes more established in our culture it throws down a number of challenges to the church.

The traditional sermon is very often 'left brained' in that it is essentially verbal rather than visual; logical and sequential in its structure; often abstract and conceptual rather than relational, concrete, experiential. The sermon is also a message which is 'given' by the preacher; the listener has no opportunity to skip the bits that are not relevant to him, or to dwell on the more useful areas and explore them in greater depth. A sermon also requires concentration in an age where TV remote controls and Internet hyperlinks are shortening everyone's attention span.

All this suggests that we may need some radical rethinking about our teaching methods if we are going to be able to communicate in a way that people are adapted to.

Living community

On a more positive note, Internet thinking challenges the passivity of the television age; it encourages engagement, participation, taking initiatives. These may help the church to make the transition (already underway) from traditional models of speaker/audience and clergy/laity towards more biblical models of 'living community', the priesthood of all believers.

If the church is able to embrace new ways of communicating which are more visual, more participatory, might not this open up a new potential for reaching the huge non-book sections of our society who have been largely untouched for decades? Maybe this is part of the answer in helping the church in this country to break out of its middle-class enclave and reach the poor.

Hidden dangers of cyberthought?

If new ways of thinking, influenced by the Internet and also by the CD-ROM, open up new possibilities and challenges, are there not some outright dangers too? Obviously we're looking here at long-term changes, so our thoughts can only be speculative. Nevertheless, to be forewarned is to be forearmed.

One thing that should prompt our concern is that the Internet (and the CD-ROM) puts the computer user in absolute control. He has the power to click the mouse on whatever he wants, whenever he wants, all the time. He need never face uncomfortable realities; if he doesn't like what he finds, he can click and move on. This seems very likely to encourage a culture of self-centredness and a living style centred on the comfort zone. It's true that sometimes a traditional sermon can be boring, but do we want to replace it with Internet sermons where people can choose only what they want to hear, never facing the truth that challenges them, makes them uncomfortable? And do we risk losing something from our learning experience when we are no longer following a direction, a logical sequence? The message of Christianity has at its heart a commitment to pleasing God and other people before self, and it gives primacy to truth above comfort; to sacrifice above gratification. The Internet puts you in control, but the Christian message is that we are to surrender our control, to place God on the throne of our lives.

The 'buzz' culture

Our society is already moving towards a 'buzz' culture. Many people have no clear perception of moral absolutes, and are facing a world where everything changes, where nothing is certain. This promotes an attitude of living for the moment, doing whatever gives you a 'buzz' at the time, whatever makes you feel good, whether it be drugs, alcohol, violence or casual sex. Will the Internet promote this philosophy, allowing people to go from one momentary 'hit' to the next? What room does this leave for Christian values of self-discipline and commitment?

Anything goes

Connection to the Internet gives immediate access to the values of just about every different culture, to almost every form of human behaviour, to ideas, views and opinions as diverse and numerous as the stars. Just what will the impact of this be? Perhaps it will accelerate the prevailing attitudes of 'anything goes' and 'whatever you're into'. Perhaps it will promote a relativist view of morality, where everyone assumes the right to define their own moral code where what's true for you need not be true for me. Perhaps at a deeper level, exposure to such a mass of ideas, information and values, all of which are constantly changing, will create a future shock of meaninglessness and disorientation.

The effect of new technology on our moral codes is not simply speculation; it has already begun to have an impact. No one knows the true extent of computer fraud, since computer companies have no wish to advertise their vulnerabilities, but everyone is agreed that it is increasing. Interestingly, many of those who have been caught have no previous criminal records and in all other respects are upright citizens. It seems that in their minds, their fraudulent activity was not acknowledged as stealing, first because the target was a large organisation rather than a person, and therefore 'legitimate'; and secondly because the crime was perpetrated indirectly via computer. These factors seem to have created a double veil, separating the fraudster from moral reality. On a similar theme, the development of the Internet means that the potential damage by computer hackers is increasing exponentially. Again, this is often perceived as 'mischief' rather than serious criminal damage.

In this environment of moral confusion, the Christian

message of hope and absolutes of truth and morality will increasingly stand apart. For some it will seem even more irrelevant than now; for many, we must hope it will be the radical alternative they desperately seek.

Summary

The Internet promotes new ways of thinking, tapping the potential of the right brain. This can be immensely satisfying, and can also generate highly productive activity. The church is in the communication business, and must therefore respond to these changes. If it succeeds in doing so, it may open up exciting new possibilities. In the longer term there may be some negative aspects to the new ways in which our society thinks, and the church needs to be aware of these.

CHAPTER 11

Cyberreality

Is the Internet creating a world in which people lose the ability to distinguish between reality and the cyberworld? Will people withdraw from reality into a virtual reality of their own construction? Are we even clear on what we mean by 'reality'?

Every person's reality is different

Reality is a strange thing. Every person's 'reality' is different. I can never fully understand how others see me or how others see themselves. I cannot ever fully comprehend what life must be like for another person, which is why the dreadful words 'I know just how you feel' are exposed in all their shallowness in a counselling situation. The words should be banned. All they show is the lack of human understanding of the speaker. I can never know exactly how another person feels. I can try to understand. I can look to similar experiences I have been through myself to help make sense of their situation, but our realities will always be different. Real empathy comes from compassionate listening rather than from pigeonholing someone else's experiences.

Reality relates to perception

Reality is therefore related to perception. At the scene of an accident or a crime there may be many witnesses. When called to give evidence in a court of law, each of the witnesses may have a contradictory account. What is the truth? Who is telling the truth and who is lying? Marriages that end in separation and divorce constitute another situation where it can be hard to establish all the rights and wrongs.

We are told that the word of God is alive and active, sharper than any two-edged sword, piercing to the division of joints and marrow, discerning the thoughts and intentions of the heart (Hebrews 4:12). We are also told by Paul in 2 Timothy 3:16–17 that all Scripture is inspired by God and is useful for teaching, correction and training in righteousness. Scripture is to be our ultimate authority in all matters of faith and conduct. Yet those Scriptures have come to us via human agents. Hence the different points of view of the Gospel writers, and the different emphasis each brings to their account of the life, ministry, death and resurrection of Jesus.

This in no way detracts from the fundamental truth of the historical accounts that God became flesh in human form in the person of Jesus around 2,000 years ago; that he taught, did miracles, suffered and died to redeem humankind; that he rose again and is now with his Father in heaven. The different perceptions of the Gospel writers, their individual realities, if you will, create a richness in their diversity. We come closer to seeing God's reality by looking towards it from four different angles. This is presumably why God ordered things so that we should have four separate Gospel records, and not just a collective summary.

Different expressions of reality point us to God

Thus one may conclude that any aspect of human experience, however removed from the temporal experience of others, may be an expression of reality for that person. Are these different aspects of our existence just different dimensions that point us to the ultimate reality that is outside space and time – the reality of a benevolent Prime-Mover, Creator, Holy God and loving Father?

The Internet has much to teach us about God, not just

through the messages on web-pages or the interaction of humans connected to it, but through the nature of the medium itself: the elements of universality and omnipresence, for example.

Prayer: another form of reality?

If we are examining the nature of reality, prayer raises some interesting issues. Prayer defies time–space logical explanation. We do not know why God has chosen to link the release of his power on earth to the requests of those who believe. Of course there are many times when he chooses to act without our prayers, and others where he chooses not to act despite them. But Jesus taught that there was a strong link.

How fast do prayers travel? What is the transmission medium? Is prayer like an e-mail, passing through the ether from ourselves to the mind of God? Is there a 'p-mail' system when God implants a thought into a prayerful human mind? What is the mechanism by which the Holy Spirit teaches us and calls to mind all Jesus has told us (John 14:26)? What is the time delay between the expression of a request to God in the mind of a believer and the effect of the answer? Are some prayers out of time-synch? Is it possible for someone to pray that God will help a friend pass a driving test at 11.00 am, forgetting that the test took place at 9.30? Can God deal with that type of prayer, either by anticipating it or by somehow altering the scheme of things?

Whatever your own model of prayer, I often think of prayer for a friend in another nation as triggering the release of a guided cruise missile of loving support and help around from one part of the world to another at more than the speed of light, filled with all the power of God himself. This is a remarkable thing.

Premonitions or intuitive understanding of the present or future is not uncommon among Christians – for example, being woken in the night with a feeling to pray urgently for a particular person, only to learn some days or weeks later that at that moment he or she had been involved in a terrible car crash. We do not know how these things work, whether they are always a direct result of God's intervention in communicating something to us, or whether in the world he created there are various extra-sensory mechanisms which we become aware of from time to time, or whether both are part of the unseen world in which we live.

Another dimension beyond our understanding

One thing is clear. As Christians we know that there is far more to this limited time–space world than meets the eye. There is a whole dimension to reality far beyond what we normally touch, see or hear. Paul tells us not to fix our eyes on what is seen but on what is unseen, for what is seen passes away, while that which is unseen is eternal (2 Corinthians 4:18). But what do we see when we fix our eyes on the unseen?

The recognition that there is another unseen dimension should temper any discussions about reality versus virtual reality. An atheist and a believer may profoundly disagree about what the ultimate reality is anyway. For me as a believer the ultimate reality is what is left when we die, when we see our Maker face to face. At the moment we see only through a veil darkly, but one day we will see face to face (1 Corinthians 13:12). Then we will be faced with the ultimate reality.

We see, then, that not only is each person's reality unique to themselves, but that all human reality is but a shadow of God's ultimate reality. This realisation should cause us to eschew strident pronouncements on what is to be classified as true reality and what is virtual reality.

Mental illness – losing touch with reality

All discussions about reality can produce reactions borne out of fear in some people, particularly those who have had the traumatic experience of caring for someone they love who has lost touch with reality through mental illness of some kind.

Psychosis can be a terrible thing when a person can no longer distinguish between the real and the imagined. Delusions of various kinds can be overwhelming, terrifying and distressing, not only for those unfortunate enough to experience them, but also for observers. Fortunately most kinds of psychosis will respond in time to proper treatment, but there is still the fear that somehow a medium like the Internet could trigger severe mental disturbances.

Unfortunately mental illness is very common, and a proportion of those using the Net will become mentally unwell every year. Around one in a hundred of all Internet users will develop schizophrenia in their lifetime and more than one in ten will need psychiatric help at some point – simply because by the law of averages that is what one would expect of any large category of people.

The commonest reason for needing psychiatric help is because of a mood change, usually depression. I am not talking here of a reactive depression where there is sadness related to a particular event such as a bereavement or loss of some other kind. I am talking about a pathological condition. But depression itself is often related to an over-gloomy interpretation of reality. The person is unable to see life as he or she would normally, and as others do. A key element in recovery can be helping the person to re-establish a more balanced view of themselves and the world.

Mental illness is also common in cyberspace

So, by the law of averages, there could be 400,000 people with schizophrenia or likely to develop it who are users of the Net at the moment (out of around 40 million) and perhaps a further 400,000 or more online who are currently needing psychiatric help.

One may argue that those who are mentally unwell may be less likely to use the Net, but you could also argue the opposite quite convincingly. We can debate the estimates, but the point is that many users are likely to have unusual or unstable mental states, and others are likely to be in great need of psychiatric help. We must take care before blaming the Internet for the mental state of such people, even if the Internet becomes tied up in some complex way with bizarre mental processes.

It is the same with faith. Someone who is a believer who becomes psychotic (perhaps as a result of a hormonal imbalance or some other biochemical problem which responds to medication) may come out with all kinds of strange ideas mixed up with faith and the church. One would not blame spirituality nor the teachings of the church for the situation. So we must take care over blaming the Internet. There will doubtless be all kinds of sensational stories about how too much time on the Internet sent so and so mad, but they may not be medically watertight.

Internet may damage those who are on the edge

It is true that if someone is in a highly vulnerable mental state, then the Internet may not do that person any good at all. One can easily see that a virtual reality world with an assumed identity could be extremely confusing to someone who is struggling to hold on to any semblance of reality anyway. One can also see that a virtual reality game involving extreme violence or degrading sexual activities could help 'normalise' and justify such behaviour in the mind of someone at the very edge of committing a major offence.

Summary

Concerns about the impact of the Internet on our perceptions of reality inevitably raise questions about the nature of reality itself. The Bible teaches us that the only true reality is in Christ. Human reality is unique to each person, based on our perceptions. Our reality is constantly being shaped, not only by 'real life', but the imaginary worlds we encounter in novels, films and even dreams. Is Internet reality any more 'virtual' than these experiences?

Nevertheless, the highly absorbing nature of the Internet, and its ability to impact us in a variety of ways, may form a particularly powerful alternative to real life that could be destabilising to certain personality types. The incidence of mental illness is such that inevitably some Internet users will become unwell, but we should be careful about making the jump from association to causation.

CHAPTER 12

Cyberrelationships

Alternative visions

Even the very word cyberrelationships might conjure up visions of a future where people hardly ever meet any more, only communicating through computer keyboards, living in an isolated world of their own, cut off from reality. But is that really the future? Or is there an alternative vision, where we can embrace the new communication potential of the Internet to help us cope with a world which is rapidly changing? I want to explore another global trend which, together with the electronic revolution, will impact the lives of growing numbers in every church in developed countries: globalisation through travel.

Travel is the world's greatest industry

Travel (including tourism) is the world's largest industry, employing 204 million people, 10.6% of the total global workforce, with a turnover of $3.4 trillion a year, growing 6.1% annually. China is building fifty major airports simultaneously and most rapid growth is occurring in the Pacific Basin. The two key words behind it all are 'relationship' and 'presence'.

Together with exploding world travel we have freedom of capital and goods on a scale never seen before, so that companies research in one continent, make goods in another and market them in another. Take computer companies, for example. They made chips in Japan, then places like Thailand, then Vietnam – constantly moving factory sites as labour costs began to rise in each country.

The speed of change is breathtaking in every area of manufacturing. Executives are struggling to keep up.

Deregulation and global corporations

Deregulation has allowed the formation of ever larger global corporations – often with mixed interests. For example, a British electricity company may now be owned by a French group, while a Canadian water company might also own a gas distribution network in Germany. Even greater shake-ups have taken place in the financial services sector, with new banks being launched every week somewhere in the world, together with rapid mergers and take-overs and the loss of tens of thousands of jobs.

Young executives today are faced with pressures to be constantly globe-trotting, or risk being left behind. In a sharply competitive labour market the choices are often bleak. Things may not be any easier if the person decides to relocate, because it is just as likely that he or she may still have to commute back to the original place where they were working on a regular basis, and all the other international trips may remain the same.

Few church leaders prepared for globalisation

Few church leaders seem fully prepared for the onslaught of globalisation and what it is going to mean. Of course large numbers of jobs will remain relatively unchanged. For example, doctors and nurses, train drivers, postal workers, retailers, designers, electricians, lawyers and dentists all have skills which will service a local population, however many others move in or out of the area. For them, unemployment will cause them to search around locally, or at worst within the same country. Others are making decisions to be downwardly mobile; to settle for less money and a slower, more relational lifestyle.

But for the frequent traveller, life is likely to become more disjointed – unless the costs of air travel soar in the future with an unexpected fuel famine, or unless international airline terrorism on a large scale means that executives become reluctant to take the risk. In the meantime, the Internet offers churches an ideal way to create new models and forums for fellowship, helping offset some of the problems of mobilisation of the workforce.

Keeping in touch

People can pray together on the Net or study the same Bible passage or offer each other emotional support. People can become e-mail pen-friends, or just use the Net to keep in touch. Globalisation of the workforce means that many churches will need to use the Internet to enable basic fellowship and friendship to be maintained.

In my own church we have a situation where a number of people are travelling internationally on a frequent basis. I have counselled one couple I know to go online as soon as possible so they can keep in touch with each other, not just friends. They both fly many times a year to different countries as far apart as the US, India and Hong Kong.

Sitting in hotels on the other side of the world

Their schedules often fail to coincide, which means that they can both be stuck in hotel rooms the other side of the world in different time zones. One is awake and the other is asleep or in meetings. When the other returns to the hotel the time has passed for a decent chat on the phone. Practical things could be set up on the Internet to help. But how common is this sort of lifestyle?

The answer is that this pattern is becoming more widespread, despite the increasing availability of alternatives such as video conferencing. Indeed it is a paradox that while more and more people are enjoying virtual reality encounters in cyberspace, there is also a yearning for reality. Human face-to-face relationships are increasingly important in a world which is fractured and urbanised.

Internet support for married couples

I suggested to this couple in our church that they both set up their own Internet accounts, and use their own portable computers to e-mail each other when on the move. I have also suggested that they invest in a couple of Internet golf-ball video cameras so that even when they are unable to talk direct, they can send each other video letters also via e-mail. And if they are fortunate enough to be in at the same time in different hotel rooms, and both have local Internet access, they could even try a long-distance Internet phone call or video conference at local call rates. We will see what happens, but the point is that keeping in touch with globalised people requires a globalised solution.

In my church we are also in the process of setting up an e-mail travel diary, listing the itineraries of various people so that at least we can pray for each other when scattered around the world – yes I am globalised too, through international lecturing. So here we have a situation where a number of people in the church are about to set up a cybersupport group for each other.

We have discussed trying to set up regular support meetings in the flesh, but schedules mean it may never happen on a regular basis – except in cyberspace. One reason we are not quite there yet is that all of us are still major fax addicts, and use e-mail far less frequently. That is changing, and when most of us find that we are checking our e-mail boxes as often as our in tray for faxes, then we will find almost overnight that a very efficient global support system will slip into place. It also requires a little setting up, with directories of e-mail numbers clustered together on each person's machine. We will be there before long.

A cyberclub for globalised Christian travellers?

The interesting thing is that once such a prayer and support network is established, it is easy to see how it could grow. After all, how about extending it to other globalised travellers in our mother church, or to other Christian friends? We might find that before long we have created an invitation-only cyberclub.

I guess in that case our only meetings might be a weekly rendezvous in a club house we build on a street in a virtual reality town somewhere. We could enjoy fellowship together with whoever is able to make it, wherever they are in the world. It would be more enjoyable if cable modems allowed us to create a five-way or ten-way video link, a cyberparty. Perhaps we should book a date now for some three years hence.

Fellowship between strangers

As we have seen, close relationships can easily develop between complete strangers on the Net. A Christian couple recently struck up a Net relationship, became cyberfriends, proposed and got married. They met physically for the first time just a week before the marriage ceremony.

In a sense this is merely an extension of traditional penfriends, although such things seem to have gone out of fashion. Similarly, someone may write to a church denominational office or to a Christian enquiry centre asking for advice. A regular correspondence may develop over a number of years and a meaningful relationship may result, where the two people begin to feel that in some ways they know each other quite well. The film *84 Charing Cross Road* gave a charming example of how two people, in this case an American author and a British bookseller, can feel they know each other even though they have never met. The Internet can take this a stage further.

Virtual reality friends

As I described in Chapter 2 there are many virtual reality worlds where you can explore a cybercity or spaceship represented by an avatar you have selected. Here you can strike up cyberfriendships, interacting with other avatars whose 'owner' may be anywhere in the world. At present, interaction is still fairly basic. Communication takes place by typing messages which appear on the screen, with some time delay and therefore not always in the right order. But it seems likely that before long this will be replaced by live speech or at the very least a voice synthesiser that converts incoming text messages to speech through your loudspeakers.

All this may sound bizarre, but how would we feel if a group of Christians decided to have some fun building their own church as a meeting place? Maybe soon there will be an area of the VR world I visit which has been taken over by a whole group of believers who are running evangelistic coffee shops, counselling sessions, and debating various subjects with whoever drops by.

Virtual sensations

As technology develops, what is there to stop these virtual friendships becoming more and more realistic? It's not hard to imagine inviting another person in the virtual world to a virtual concert hall to listen to music. Probably there will soon be the capacity for replacing the avatars with more accurate representations of yourself using photographs. With virtual reality suits it would be possible to hold hands with someone who is on the other side of the globe. What are the implications of this for relationships?

The trust gap

No matter how far virtual reality technology develops there will always be a crucial gap: trust. This is because in Internet relationships, people can pretend in a way which is difficult or near impossible if you know them well in the flesh. In the situation where e-mail is received from an unknown person, the receiver has no guarantee that anything said by the writer is true because there are no means whatever of verification. The person's name could also be false, their whole identity and persona a complete fiction. While such things do happen, and also occur in face-to-face encounters, they are very unusual. Just as well, or the whole of social interaction would collapse under the burden of mutual suspicion.

Internet anonymity

The Internet has bred a certain culture of anonymity, partly as a protection against the unknown terrors of cyberspace. After all, on Internet Relay Chat anyone might be listening from any part of the world and you might never know, because they too have made themselves anonymous. The culture of pornography has also encouraged many people to have web addresses and names that are difficult to trace to actual people with addresses and telephone numbers, so they can browse with impunity. It is true therefore that you are far more likely to be in for a surprise on the Net than in the ordinary world.

An example might be someone purporting to be a vulnerable fifteen-year-old girl asking for advice from a church e-mail box about child abuse, when the person is really a fifty-year-old man with deep personal problems who gains some kind of strange satisfaction out of such behaviour. On the Net there is a saying: 'You never know if you are talking to the dog.'

Virtual adultery

Relationships can develop in cyberspace which are very unhealthy. An obvious example might be a paedophile pretending to be a child, aiming to persuade a child to reveal her name and address. Another example might be a married man or a married woman who is spending time talking into the night with someone of the opposite sex. There was a recent example where an Internet friend was cited in a divorce case as a contributor to the breakdown of a marriage. The wife discovered a whole string of very explicit and intimate e-mail letters, and the marriage was over.

The question is whether it is possible to commit 'virtual adultery'; to be unfaithful with someone one has never met. The biblical perspective of marriage is is that it brings a man and woman into a special union: 'For this reason a man will leave his father and mother and be united to his wife, and they will become one flesh' (Genesis 2:24).

Jesus uses the same language but develops it further, adding, 'So they are no longer two but one' (Matthew 19:5–6). This union has spiritual and emotional dimensions as well as the physical.

And so does Paul, in his teaching about marriage: 'Do you not know that he who unites himself with a prostitute is one with her in body? For it is said, "The two will become one flesh"' (1 Corinthians 6:16).

Thus we are taught that union has a spiritual dimension as well as an emotional and physical one.

Cybersex is already on offer

It's vital that we have a clear understanding of these biblical principles. As virtual reality technology develops, Internet relationships might indeed acquire a sexual dimension. Indeed, many adult sites already boast of that possibility – a new variation on virus-free safer sex. At present all they are marketing is some kind of interactive video link, but all kinds of further virtual dimensions will doubtless eventually be offered, probably using virtual touch and other sensations.

All kinds of strange relationships could develop in a virtual world, with people selecting bodies for themselves that fit their own fantasies of what they wish they looked like, attracted to each other on the basis of a fantastical appearance, a mythical projection. What if VR programs designed to help people build their own buildings were adapted to simulate images of live body-to-body interactions? There is at least one adult site on the Net which is trying to incorporate sensation as part of their cybersex offerings. What will be the situation in ten years' time when perhaps extended body suits are available?

From the Christian point of view the situation is clear: all of these things are impossible to reconcile with the historic and traditional teachings of the church based on the Scriptures and 2,000 years of church teaching, to the effect that believers are called to celibacy or monogamous marriage.

Emotional betrayal

Even if cybersex is still some way off, it is still possible to commit emotional adultery if a person pours out his or her heart in an intimate way, depriving a spouse of that intimacy. Such behaviour would not justify a separation, but it would be unhelpful at best and emotionally unfaithful at worst. Jesus also taught that it is possible to commit adultery in one's heart when he talked about the power of fantasy: 'But I tell you that anyone who looks at a woman lustfully has already committed adultery with her in his heart' (Matthew 5:28).

It is possible to develop an intense relationship with someone in a way which seriously weakens and undermines a marriage. One may never have met the person in the flesh but, as we have seen, the power of the Internet to create feelings of great intimacy should never be underestimated – and that is in an Internet world with just e-mail and relay chat, with no video or telephone links.

Relationship guidelines for cyberspace

We need an ethical code to guide us in cyberspace relationships, helping define the acceptable, the marginal, the questionable and the spiritually suicidal. A helpful and simple starting point would be to say that whatever one would feel comfortable or not comfortable doing in normal day-to-day life is probably a reasonable guide to go by in cyberspace. The only rider to this is that cyberspace is a far more friendly place than the street in which you or I may live, and there are all kinds of basic level friendships which can develop in a very helpful and healthy way which would never happen outside the world of the Net. At the same time, there are great unknowns about the real lives of people one meets, and one needs to take care.

Unreal relationships with real people

Having said all this we need to be careful of drawing too great a distinction between the dangers of virtual relationships and those we encounter in real life. Virtual relationships are just as real in some ways as relationships in the flesh, because by definition they are relationships with real people, even if they are lived through an unreal situation. A relationship with real people in an unreal situation could be just as apt a description for other circumstances we experience in ordinary life, such as encounters on a business trip abroad, a singles holiday, or a state of war.

Many situations take us out of our normal context and place us in an environment which feels detached from normal reality, and one where we can find ourselves behaving in a way which would be unthinkable back home. To a mild degree this is a healthy part of rest and recreation, but several steps on from there can be danger and a terrible mistake.

The need to breathe the same air

For most people, the likelihood of developing an unhealthy or damaging relationship is far greater in real life than it is in cyberspace. There is something very important about breathing the same air, being in the same room, which is self-evident when you look at the pull of live theatre or concert performances. A live relay to a big screen in an auditorium next door is not the same thing at all, nor is a film of the performance shown on a wide screen. Something is missing. There is a spiritual, intangible element to human interaction which evades logical analysis. It is the secret of the charismatic communicator; the reason why one actor is paid ten thousand times more than another.

Hunger for reality

This then is the reverse side of the coin. Even as we rush headlong into the techno-world, our fractured society with its isolation and loss of community generates a still greater yearning for satisfying relationships, for genuine human contact. It seems that exposure to simulation only provokes us to seek out the reality. It is interesting that in a culture dominated by television, people want to travel more, not less. Images on a screen don't satisfy our appetite, they just whet it for the real thing. No amount of electronic trickery can take away the desire to be there: to smell the air, to hear the sounds of the busy street, to feel the fur of an unusual animal, to watch a strange butterfly soar in the breeze, to feel the bruised and worn banknotes of a foreign currency and to try the taste of unfamiliar food.

Summary

In summary, then, the Net is ideal as a medium for having fellowship with people you know who may be many thousands of miles away. As we move towards a global economy, the Internet may be a lifesaver to marriages, and a way in which a pastor can maintain contact with members of his congregation who are overseas, or who are simply working shifts that preclude them from attending meetings regularly.

The Internet may be a means of forming new relationships with people from all over the world. But given the anonymity of the Net, there will always be a need for caution. Cyberintimacy can develop, and there is a need to guard against damaging relationships, although for most people the risk is probably greater with real-life situations.

The Internet can never be a full substitute for normal human interaction and experience.

CHAPTER 13

Conclusions

Cyberchurch – is it biblical?

It may seem strange to some, after all that has gone before, to formally ask the question whether the Internet is biblical. The fact is that there are many things that we take for granted in a modern society for which no 'proof-texts' can be found, and other things that many Christians are opposed to which are not condemned by any specific Bible verses.

Proof-texts for technology

An example of an issue without proof-texts to guide us is that of genetic engineering. Scientists are now adding human genes to cows, pigs, sheep, rabbits and fish for various purposes, creating new types of animals. There are scriptural principles that can be deduced, such as that humans are made in God's image, but we struggle to find a charter for biotechnology in the Bible. What about mixing sheep and goats to make geep – or horses and donkeys to make mules for that matter? What about gene screening for disease in adults or gene insertions to produce better crops for developing countries?

Many other ethical ambiguities are found when it comes to information technology. One may take the position that technological progress is morally neutral, and that it is the use we make of the opportunities it affords that creates the moral questions. How do we evaluate those opportunities? As Christians, even where we lack clear proof-texts, we must seek to weigh them against the principles God gives us in Scripture. Interestingly, when we do so we find some notable parallels.

Paul was the first cyberapostle

Paul was the first cyberapostle. His overwhelming desire was always to be present personally with a local church, but when in prison he used all the communication technology at his disposal to make himself virtually present throughout the known world.

The technology he used, pen and ink, was not universally understood, for many were illiterate. It was state-of-the-art in his day. Through a scribe, he was able to give similar teachings across the churches, as other writers duplicated the message. In one case a personal letter written from one human to another (Paul to Timothy) was eavesdropped on by thousands all over the known world. The technology also allowed Paul to be virtually present in different eras, a hundred years later, even 2,000 years later.

As we have seen, in many ways the Internet is no different from any other medium. The Internet makes a big and chaotic world seem smaller and more intimate, but so does every other form of communication. It turns a globalised existence into a village again. In and of itself the Internet is morally neutral.

Internet broadcasts the word of God

Scripture tells us that the word of the Lord falls on the earth like rain from the sky and never returns without accomplishing its purpose (Isaiah 55:10–11). The Internet is just another way of broadcasting that word. From the time of Moses onwards, the written word became a primary means by which the truth of God was communicated. Ever since Moses returned from Mount Sinai carrying two large stones engraved with the Ten Commandments, the written law began to have force that would only be qualified after the coming of Jesus himself.

There were two key factors that enabled the early

believers to carry their message so fast: one is mobility, and the other is common language. Both these factors are directly relevant to any discussion about the biblical basis for using the Internet.

Mobility and common language help the gospel

Mobility is a factor we tend to take for granted in studying the New Testament, but that is a serious mistake. It was H.G. Wells in his *Short History of the World* who pointed out that if a human mind had planned the coming of Jesus at any point in history over the last 4,000 years, barring the last century, then it would probably have chosen the Middle East at the time of the Roman Empire. Superb road communications had been created at vast cost by battalions of Roman soldiers, which made the dissemination of the gospel so rapid. Jesus was born and lived in a narrow area which was a main artery of international trade for the entire known world. Today the information superhighway is the ultimate mobility system, allowing you and me to be 'transported' around the world at incredible speed.

However, common language was also vital. The Greek Empire of Alexander the Great had left a legacy of fluent Greek among a vast population that later became the Roman Empire. Hence Paul could write a letter in Greek (not the Latin language of the Romans), confident that he would be understood by the membership of the churches in every nation.

Global language is a tool for the gospel

Today the universal language is English, used now in 60% of world broadcasts, 70% of world mail, 85% of international calls and 80% of all computer data. English is the dominant language of the Net, vastly greater in influence than any other tongue.

Computer languages have become standard too. After the battles for personal computer supremacy in the early

1980s, IBM managed to set a global standard for all manufacturers, even though it lost most of the market share. As a result, over a decade later almost every personal computer produced is still identical in basic architecture – apart from Apple's Macintosh computers.

Boards and chips can be taken from one manufacturer's machine and plugged into another fairly routinely. The software too has become standard. Microsoft managed to do a deal with IBM, allowing one of the most successful monopolies in history to develop. The Microsoft operating system MS-DOS, followed by *Windows* and then *Windows 95*, has been sold with almost every PC made since 1983.

However, hundreds of thousands of far larger computer systems used other operating systems such as UNIX. Then along came the Internet and browser programs, which run in almost identical ways, whatever the size or type of computer system. Thus the student attached to a massive UNIX super-computer sees the same web-sites in the same way as a user at home on a conventional desk-top PC running *Windows*.

Therefore we now have not only a common text language, but also a common computer language available to connect the Net to every computer in the whole world. Both these events have only developed in the last decade. The relevance of this is profound. Just as it is easy to forget the impact of the Greek and Roman Empires on the mass evangelisation of the known world after the resurrection of Jesus, it is easy today to underrate the significance of a global language and a global information system.

From this perspective we can see that the Internet is reproducing many of the conditions that were highly conducive to the explosive spread of the gospel in the first century.

New possibilities

I have emphasised this point all along our journey through cyberworld, that in many ways the Internet is a form of communication which differs more in degree than in principle from other forms. Even some of the deeper questions raised by the Internet – 'What is reality?'; 'What are the essentials of human relationships?'; 'What are the necessary boundaries to freedom?' – have already been posed by television and the telephone. Nevertheless, we need to recognise that in terms of sheer scale, diversity, pervasiveness and depth of impact, the Internet is a revolution. We have seen how it creates exciting possibilities for communications, relationship building, evangelism, teaching and creative approaches to prayer and worship; how it opens up new horizons in research and pastoral care; how it creates new challenges as we seek to communicate the message of the gospel to a society that is even learning to think in new ways.

New dangers

We have seen, on the other hand, how the Internet has its dangers that can affect Christians directly, or about which we should be deeply concerned when we see them impacting the society around us: the risk of addiction, exposure to pornography and subversive materials; potentially damaging relationships; losing touch with reality.

In Romans 12:2 Paul warns: 'Don't let the world around you squeeze you into its own mold' (J.B. Phillips). Throughout this book I have argued that the presence of risks and problems calls us to a greater involvement rather than to withdrawal. We need to be at the forefront of these developments; to be the shapers, not the shaped.

I have also argued that for all its potential, the Internet can never replace face-to-face human relationships – never be a substitute for fellowship and Christian community. But not everyone will take this view. The same doors that open up new possibilities for enhancing community also create the possibility of cyberChristians. They may believe, they may worship, they may attend cyberchurches to which they tithe; they may have cyberfellowship and study the Bible. But they choose, for whatever reason, never to meet together with other Christians. What is our response to this?

Meeting together

It is extremely difficult to square a biblical view of Christianity with any teaching that suggests it is tolerable to encourage Christians that they do not need to meet together 'in the flesh' (albeit in the Spirit too!). One could go further and say that any group which promoted such an idea was likely to lead people astray and weaken a fundamental teaching of the church.

I can remember a few years ago when a new influence of ultra-radical teaching hit the city where I live. The idea was that you did not need to go to church to be a Christian. It went further than this to create a positive climate where people who had been committed church members felt that they could stop attending any church meetings. Discussions were difficult. They declared that very few scriptures, apart from Hebrews 10:24, explicitly commanded believers to meet.

The outcome was very upsetting. A family left the church. Cut off from all fellowship by their own withdrawal from almost all social contact, they gradually drifted away from faith altogether. They were gripped by a false doctrine which wrecked them. Such a doctrine could have destroyed the church completely, were it not for the fact that the vast majority of the congregation had foundations for their lives based not on isolated proof-texts, but on the whole sweep of biblical truth from Genesis to Revelation.

Local church membership

My concern is that such a theology could emerge again, linked to the Internet, claiming that cybermeetings are a full, complete and sufficient expression of the body of Christ and that attending cyberchurch meetings absolves people from any obligation to meet other believers locally for worship, teaching or prayer 'in the flesh'. Incidentally, they would have to deal with issues such as baptism and breaking bread together, as well as other witnessed ceremonies such as marriage.

So, then, cyberchurch as a complete church in the conventional sense seems to me impossible to justify from Scripture, however realistic the virtual reality links may become, and however many people may be joined simultaneously.

Compassion, not judgement

Having said that, as we have already seen, there are times when many believers are not able to meet because of travel, shift-working, sickness, location, persecution or imprisonment. Or they may suffer from agoraphobia, or hang-ups caused by being poorly treated by churches in the past. All I am saying here is that we should beware being judgemental. Cyberbelievers need love too. We may not like the way in which they seem to reject conventional church activity, but they still belong to God.

Some may argue that such people are not Christians at all, because if they were they would attend a local church. But the apostle Paul's words are a rebuke: 'If on your lips is the confession that Jesus is Lord and in your heart the faith that Jesus rose from the dead then you will find salvation' (Romans 10:9, New English Bible). However, John's letters also tell us that a test of discipleship is obedience to what Jesus has said, and as we have seen, gathering for worship, prayer and teaching seems to have been fundamental to the New Testament understanding of what it is to follow God. But if a person is following an active and obedient path in every other area, what then?

What about the tens of thousands of believers across the world who attend church, witness for Christ and aim to obey him, yet are mean with their money when it comes to supporting God's work; or people who do all those things and are generous financially but are unkind to their wives and children, or are bitter, resentful, gossips or just proud? Where do we draw the line? Who are we to make that final judgement?

In conclusion . . .

In conclusion, then, it is clear that as disciples of Jesus Christ we are called to love, honour and obey him in every area of our lives, using every means at our disposal to fulfil the Great Commission to go into every part of our world, make disciples in all nations, baptising and teaching people everywhere. The Internet can help us with that, as a powerful tool to reach people, to help them find faith, and to support them as believers.

The Internet can never be a proper substitute for a local community of believers, a living witness to the power of Christ, and could be an escape from the normal and healthy pressures of daily life, including the biblical command for us to love our brothers in Christ and our neighbours as ourselves – and to love those we do not naturally feel like loving, even our enemies as well.

The Christian faith is a relational gospel. The message begins with an understanding of a relational God revealed to us as Father, Son and Holy Spirit, three in one. The Bible narrative is of a Creator God who has made people in his own image to have relationship with him; of a God who is grieved when people's imperfections make communion with him impossible without his rescue plan in the person of Jesus.

The whole of both Old and New Testaments is dominated by the twin themes of reconciliation and restoration of relationship between God and man and between human beings. The picture of our future is a world where after the coming again of Jesus there will be an end to suffering, illness, wars and strife.

Jesus did not come to win solitary believers, but to build a church on earth as a holy nation, a royal priesthood, with a common identity, calling and purpose. We are called to serve God together, not to isolate ourselves into little islands of our own. Our worlds are made to be shared and embraced together.

If the Internet enables us to do some of these things more effectively — reaching, teaching, supporting and encouraging — then that will be a positive thing. However, if the Internet gives rise to a new cybertheology which sees cyberexistence as an end in itself, then an error will have been allowed to take root.

And finally . . . a lesson from history

Christians tend to be naturally conservative and cautious about change, but it would be tragic if we saw beyond 2000 a growing anti-technology movement which discouraged millions of believers from playing their part in shaping cyberspace.

There is an unmistakable echo from the past, from the time when printing was first invented, which resonates with the birth of the information age today. Over 500 years ago, in 1476, William Caxton set up the first English printing press in Westminster, England, having printed the first book ever to be produced in English. A few decades later, in 1522, just two years after Martin Luther's treatise against Rome, William Tyndale felt moved to translate the whole Bible into English. His aim was to use the latest printing technology to produce English Bibles for the people. The Bishop of London refused to support the idea and Tyndale went to Germany, finishing the task at Hamburg.

The first translation was printed a few pages at a time in Cologne in 1525, but production was halted by magistrates before a single copy was complete. The Bibles were finally produced in Worms the following year. Tyndale's translation had to be smuggled into England, such was the opposition by church leaders to the idea not only of a Bible widely available in the mother tongue, but also one translated from the original Hebrew and Greek rather than the Latin Vulgate text.

Many died to see Bibles printed. Tyndale's work cost him his life. In 1535 he was arrested near Antwerp and imprisoned. This was a very significant period in the history of the church. Forces of regeneration were growing. While Tyndale was in prison John Calvin printed the first version of his revolutionary teachings. Tyndale was strangled and burned at the stake on 6 October 1536.

The combination of new printing technology and availability of a good English Bible translation had a huge impact on the English speaking church. Until that time the Bible was only available as a handwritten manuscript. Copies were rare, beyond the reach of ordinary people, and were in Latin, which few apart from priests could read.

People began to read and understand the Scriptures for themselves and were amazed. Whole generations of thinkers began to form a different view of what church was about and of who Jesus was. Their own writings were also printed and became widely available. Technology greatly accelerated the process of reformation, leading to the establishment of the Protestant Church.

The technology martyrs. It is hard to imagine what kind of primitive faith would still be practised today were it not for the invention of printing. The Scriptures would still be almost unknown. It is disturbing that those who were most opposed to Bible translation, printing and distribution were leaders of the church. Many were martyred as a result for the great crime of using technology to communicate the gospel to the people in a way which they could understand, in the language of their culture. This was a movement to popularise faith.

The Internet is just a massive electronic printing press, popularising everything connected with it. We must not allow church leaders who fear it to prevent its widespread use in every possible way as a God-given means of proclamation and explanation. The Internet world needs cyberchurch, not as a substitute for local church life, but as a vibrant electronic expression of the life found in the body of Christ worldwide, as a window to faith in an increasingly fragmented and confused world. We cannot fulfil the Great Commission to go into all the world if we stay out of the cyberworld.

We are commanded to go. We are commanded to go into all the world, and that includes cyberspace (Matthew 28:19). The only questions that remain are who, what, when, where and how? The following Appendix addresses these questions, but two can be answered immediately. The answer to 'when?' is now. As a Christian community we cannot delay any further with just small experiments, although timing of individual and group involvement is critical. However, no individual or group should fall into the trap of rushing ahead without a clear call from God, or we shall just end up following the latest fad.

The answer to 'where?' is that it does not matter much, since in cyberspace everywhere is as close as your computer screen.

Postscript

by
Prabhu Guptara

Group Director, Organisational Learning and Transportation, Union
Bank of Switzerland; and Visiting Professor at various universities
and business schools.

What a dull word 'church' is. It conjures up the image of a large
piece of history, cold and empty except for museum-like
objects, beautiful maybe, but from times long ago.

What a lovely word 'church' is. It brings to mind a time of
ceremony and joy each Sunday morning.

What a hopeless word 'church' is. It can convey to most
minds either or both of these meanings without coming anywhere near what Jesus the Lord talked about when he spoke
about the church!

What did Jesus mean by 'church'? A new community of
people, freed not only from the failings of their own individual
past, but also from the failings of their family, their clan, their
tribe and their nation – free to fulfil their own potential, free to
help each other regardless of their backgrounds or their skin
colour or gender, free to re-evaluate their communal and individual histories in order to build on the best and abandon the
worst. Free to be the people that God had intended them to be.
Free to walk with God. Free to build and rebuild the world in
order to bring out all its beauty and loveliness and make it a
home fit for humans, a reflection of the glory and the love of
God himself.

In that sense, the church was always intended to be cyber.
Has always been cyber.

It was always intended to span time and space. It does span
time and place. We may not see them, but we are each of us
surrounded by a cloud of witnesses: Adam and Eve and Abra-
ham and Sarah and Matthew and indeed the Trinity watch every
moment of each person's life. I may not know the believers in
Mongolia or in the next street but they are part of our community, part of the church.

And for us as a community, the question is: do we dare to live our lives on the basis of Jesus' teaching about community which cuts across all barriers including those of time and space, or are we going to continue to be limited by the understanding of the church as a merely local building or only a local body, which comes together once a week? What relationship can I, do I, have with God the Father whom I cannot see, or with Jesus the Lord whom I cannot see, or with the Holy Spirit whom I cannot see, or with the apostles whom I cannot see, or with believers to whom and with whom I cannot be physically present? What does it mean to be physically present anyway, in an age when I can be present as a photograph or even as a living and moving image on a screen? What was perhaps merely theory or something only mystics took seriously, has after all these years become more of a reality. More of a question with which we need to wrestle. We could say that the IT revolution is only the latest in a series of steps (including such things as cars and aeroplanes and telephones and radio and television) which, in spite of their negative side-effects, have been and are being used by God to help us to a fuller understanding of what Jesus means by 'church'.

Patrick's book is an enormous help in this process. It provides a range of facts and ideas. It raises a number of questions.

One of the kinds of questions he raises relates to the *nature* of the Internet and whether or to what degree we should be involved with it.

A second kind of question he raises to the *contents* carried by the medium and what should be the contribution of the church to that.

The third kind of question he raises relates to the *consequences* of this new medium. Patrick focuses on the individual and church-related consequences. I believe there are other profound questions which we should at least mention, specifically in the areas of society, economics and politics.

The coming of the cybersociety will have consequences in these areas, as far as I can see, which will be as profound as the Industrial Revolution and the post-war boom combined. The Industrial Revolution, among other things, resulted in an enormous shift in the mode of society from agricultural to industrial and an enormous shift in populations from villages to cities (which continues to this day to a greater or lesser extent in different parts of the world); some people saw the change coming and seized the initiative in creating the new society, profiting in the process; others simply went along with the change; while the Luddites and other populist movements in the 1800s actively resisted the changes as long as they could. The post-war boom created a fundamental shift in attitudes and values towards materialism and individualism, opposed for a short while unsuccessfully (in a way very similar to that of the Luddites) by the Hippies. The church, as far as I can see, missed the true scale and significance of both the Industrial Revolution and the post-war boom, with consequences which are evident today in still-declining church membership and a low quality of discipleship (generally speaking) in areas of the world affected by these shifts.

The church did not, however, miss the significance of the revolution in literacy and education made possible by printing – indeed, we pioneered some of that revolution. The result of seizing the initiative then was blessing which flows down to this day in those areas.

I believe that God is giving us a fundamental choice again, not only in the area of communicating the Truth, but also in the area of contributing to the reshaping of society. We have the choice between experiencing again the blessing which followed our seizing the possibilities created (as in the case of printing) or the curse which followed our missing the possibilities (as in the case of the Industrial Revolution and the post-war boom).

Just as the coming of railways, cars and aeroplanes reshaped transport systems and city centres, so will the coming of cyber-society: city centres will be even more quickly emptied by everyone who can escape them for cheaper and more pleasant surrounding (unless authorities take radical steps to change the financial, transport and social infrastructure of towns and cities); commercial property in cities will in any case plummet in value but may gain elsewhere; the transport industry will shrink, especially within countries but even around the world as the consequences of our environmental profligacy come home to roost at the same time as 'travel' by video and virtual reality become the cheaper, stress-saving and infection-free way to do so; the retail industry will die or be gobbled up in the new mega-industries which cross traditional divisions of industry; shopping malls and real travel will be for the affluent; home-shopping will be the area where the key commercial battles are fought.

More fundamentally, the traditional job will disappear, society will be even more radically split between the 'haves' and the 'have-nots'; parliamentary democracy will be called into question for the first time in 'advanced' societies by the technological possibility of direct democracy on a massive scale. Democracy will also be called into question by the desire of the super-rich to control the resistance of the mass of population in developed countries to the blandishments of 'mega-commerce' and the 'logic of economics'; the trend towards individual isolation will be accelerated, and so on.

What will be consequences of all this for our fellowships? For evangelism? For nurture? In contrast to the fragmentation of civil society, should we begin to re-examine the notion of genuinely communal life-styles (like kibbutzim)? Democracy is popularly thought to have been a Greek notion, but it was originally biblical and has been able to be practised for longer than seventy years only in societies shaped by a Protestant worldview; in other societies, it has either never come into being, or it has been experimented with for as long as possible before those societies have collapsed into chaos or dictatorship. And it is an interesting question whether democracy can survive beyond the third or fourth generation in post-Protestant societies (we are already in the second generation, and the pressures are evident). Will world trade and the death of democracy mean the emergence of new 'protected areas', new tribes ruled by dictators whose rule is the more absolute as a result of advances in technology? In any case, the global tribes which are already developing in the cyberworld will not be reached merely by what we say by lip or computer. They will be reached only as we demonstrate a different quality of life in the way that we organise ourselves in reality.

We already have some interconnected 'Christian ghettos' on the Internet, but what they do not understand is that it is not enough to push information out into the Internet. Such information is dead unless people pull it into their computers (or 'access it' as the technical terminology has it). The information society risks becoming the first society in which the gospel is 'unac-cessed', where the Truth is, in principle, available but is never actually heard because it is perceived to be old hat, unbelievable or irrelevant. What we need is a new class of 'techno-missionaries', called by God to penetrate the territory, learn the language, win the right to be heard, and then communicate the Truth in a form which will be perceived by the inhabitants to be understandable and relevant. These techno-missionaries need to be tent-makers, or they will not be respected and therefore not be heard in the techno-jungle. The wonderful thing is that each of these techno-tribes is far more accessible, and at far less cost and sacrifice, than were the tribes of Africa or India.

It could be argued that, whereas the eighteenth-century missionary movement was healthy, it lost its way after the middle of the nineteenth century, because the real missionary task was no longer in the wilds of China or Latin America, but in the Western world itself, which was rapidly becoming shorn of Truth. As a result of ignoring the challenge at home, even the peoples who were won at great cost in countries such as Tanzania were lost again within a couple of generations – their children may have been educated in 'Christian' schools, but the brightest of them went on to Oxford and Cambridge where they lost their faith, and then returned to their countries to lead them into Marxism or materialism. By contrast, if the missionary effort had concentrated in the West after the nineteenth-century communications revolution began, we would not have needed to open schools and colleges by ourselves; the forces of modernisation from the West would have communicated the Truth implicitly and explicitly far more effectively than those schools and colleges, and the individuals and peoples would have continued serving the Truth.

The nature of the task today is clear, it is to engage in the effort of understanding and working with the forces that will tear up society as we know it, probably in the next ten years; *at the same time* as we strive to create a counter-culture which will survive the eventual breakdown of this society. This is very different from mere Pat Buchanan-style Luddism; this is parallel to the way the church became the counter-culture which survived the breakdown of the Roman Empire by absorbing, enhancing and preserving the best that the Roman Empire had to offer but in the context of a new kind of community.

We do not know what is ahead for society, economics and

politics. I have not mentioned the effects of automated manufacture and artificial intelligence and neural networks. No one knows what is ahead, except God. Who knows if we are now in the end times? Certainly, the coming of cybersociety will unleash the technical means of making real some of the things which are hinted at in the Book of Revelation. But of course Jesus taught that we should always be living as if we are in the end times, even though the exact times are known to God alone. What should mark us as a community is hope – in contrast to the people who are without Truth and therefore without hope, who are depressed when they see the changes ahead. We see the changes and, far from being afraid, we are excited because we know that it is God, our God, who shakes the foundations and does a new thing, and has all history under his control, and is finally going to end this world system and usher in the beginning of real history with the supernatural introduction of his kingdom, the new heaven and the new earth.

I believe that he has given us in the coming of the Internet a moment of profound opportunity. It offers us the possibility of communicating Truth to many millions of people in West and East, if we go about the job in something like the way we should. The keys are engagement with that opportunity, professionalism in the way we go about it, an understanding of our times, and true community.

A Practical Way Forward

So you want to experience the Net for yourself. The first question to ask is what you want to do once you are connected. You might just want to have a look around, search for useful information and also to get an e-mail box of your own or for your church. On the other hand, you may be considering becoming an information provider.

Connecting to the Net for ordinary use is very straightforward – in theory. In practice it can take some fiddling about with the settings on your machine. The first thing you need is a computer. Just about any PC can be connected, and many other kinds of computers. Many people are using old 286 or 386 machines perfectly well, although if they are using anything other than a text-only system from a provider like Delphi, then they will be very frustrated. However, you don't need a great or fast computer brain to read text as it comes down the telephone line.

The critical factor is the modem. The fastest modem you can get at the time of writing is a 28.8kbps (kilobytes per second). This is really what you need unless you are only going online occasionally, or you have all the time in the world. Having said that, the Net will work quite well with a 14.5kbps unit.

To be comfortable on the Net you need a decent amount of free disk space after installing *Windows* and all the other programs you want to use. The reason for this is that browsers (used to view pages) take up space and you will want to be able to download all kinds of free software and files. Without adequate disk space you will feel very frustrated. Ideally you need 30 megabytes minimum to be comfortable.

I started off on the Internet with just a 14.4kbps modem and a portable 386 with just 2 megabytes of RAM and 80 megabytes of hard disk, which was already full almost to bursting. It could only cope with Delphi as an Internet provider (text-based with no graphics). With no images to load it was extremely fast but limited. E-mail worked fine. That kind of low-powered hardware can probably be picked up second-hand for less than £200 including a modem if you look around and do not mind a large old computer on your desk. Such a system is now one of the seven computers in our house, two of which are on the Net, and most of which are very old.

My latest computer is a vast step up: a Pentium 133 megahertz chip with 16 megabytes RAM and 1.6 thousand million bytes (gigabytes) of hard disk storage. It is ten times as fast as my old portable bought four years ago and came fitted with a 28.8 modem, speakers, microphone and six-speed CD-ROM, able to play video at normal speed from a CD.

On the day I unpacked it one-third of the disk space disappeared with all the software that came with it and the programs I added. In the following twelve weeks another 200 megabytes disappeared. When you realise that a single photograph can occupy as much as a megabyte, you can see that the space could vanish in no time at all. Similar systems to the above could be bought for around £1,500 at the end of 1996, with prices expected to halve for the same specification roughly every twelve to eighteen months.

The next step is to connect to an Internet provider. There are a huge number of these and the list is being added to by the week. Two kinds exist: one simply provides a line onto the Net, while the other has a huge amount of information in its own site which as a member you can access for free. Examples are CompuServe, AOL and Microsoft Network. Sometimes people find that the local information is so good that they hardly bother going out onto the Net. Membership fees for these providers can be less than £6 per month.

These information providers are going out of fashion fast because the Internet is now so huge and easy to use. They are also up to twice the cost of direct Internet providers. The next question is whether you want to pay for the hours you use, or to buy a flat rate system. It is possible to buy unlimited access at the time of writing for around £100 a year. However, you need to be certain that the provider has enough capacity to cope.

Take a free tour

A good starting point is to take a free tour of a number of different systems. On many computer magazines there are free CDs or floppy disks attached to the front cover which will plug you directly into one or other of these Internet companies. In exchange for your credit card details you are given a free month of access, up to a maximum number of hours (typically ten).

So long as you cancel your subscription before you reach the limit you can sign onto another provider and repeat the process. In this way you could enjoy several months' free Internet access, and at the same time get a feel of what the different companies are offering and, most important of all, what their system response time is like, as well as their telephone back-up. For example, some companies provide telephone support seven days a week, up to 10 pm most nights, while others hardly have a service at all. Evening support is vital since that is when you are most likely to use the Net if you are taking advantage of low-cost telephone calls.

Lists of all these providers, and charts comparing what they offer, are included in many Internet magazines. Before you take the plunge, it is well worth stopping off at a large newsagent and buying several of the many Internet magazines currently available. These magazines will also give you extra advice and a list of the latest innovative sites to visit when you are online.

There are three other ways to join the Net if you cannot find a free disk. First, phone an advertised service in one of the magazines and ask them to send you a disk. Secondly, use the hyperterminal in the accessories of *Windows 95* to dial the company and then download their software – if you feel able to do that (you may need someone from the company on the phone to talk you through it). Thirdly, you can always go to a big computer store like PC World and buy a complete package, including a modem and manuals.

Many cities now have fibre optic cables laid by companies offering cable television and cable telephone services, including Internet connection. This is usually the cheapest way to get onto the Net. You will probably be able to pay a flat rate for unlimited access, and will almost certainly enjoy free calls for as long as you like to the Internet provider after a certain time on weekday evenings and all day at weekends.

Browsers

Searching for what you want is easy. On the disks you get a browser provided by the Internet user. This will enable you to find things. There is also a browser provided as standard with *Windows 95*, called *Internet Explorer*. This is now provided free to anyone who wants it. The most popular browser is *Navigator* from Netscape and can also be downloaded for free.

There are various search engines you can use. They each work and present the information in slightly different ways. The most powerful search facility is probably *Alta Vista*, which is found on the Digital site. Some search engines list what you are looking for in the frequency order in which your key words appear. Others like *Magellan* only list sites which have been inspected and reviewed and given a star rating.

Protect the children

Protecting the children is an important consideration. I recommend *Cyber-Sitter* version for *Windows 95*. However, look around as there are several similar programs and prices vary. Make sure that you keep logging onto the site to collect update files which are free after buying the program. You can also download the whole thing with a credit card number.

Some Internet service providers claim to have their own mechanisms for censoring sites. These claims should not be treated as an absolute protection. See Internet magazines for the latest details because they are changing all the time.

Virus protection and back-up

You will also want to protect your valuable system from being destroyed by computer viruses. One of the best programs is *Dr Solomon's Anti-Virus Toolkit*. It is expensive, but you get the first year's updates free and peace of mind is important. No one can insure you for the lost time of a wiped hard disk. The risk of a viral catastrophe may be as low as your home burning down, but then you insure against that.

Incidentally it is almost scandalous that powerful PCs on which a whole company's future could depend, or a university degree, or your family finances, are usually packaged with nothing better than a 1.4 megabyte floppy disk drive as a back-up in case a hard disk is damaged in some way. I would need to buy up to a thousand floppy disks just to make one copy of what is on my hard disk. Utter madness! What happens in practice is that people just use a system and hope for the best. The trouble is that even if all the documents and data files are on floppies, it can take several days of hard work to reload all the program disks, and that is assuming you can remember all the tricks you learned at the time to get them set up in the right way. A hard disk crash is a disaster under such circumstances.

The best solution is a tape streamer, which costs £100–200 and allows you to copy an entire hard disk onto one tape – a process which can be timed to happen automatically onto different tapes every day or every week. A corrupt or damaged disk can be replaced by an engineer and within a couple of hours the entire system should be running exactly as it was when the back-up was made. Internet use alters so many things on a disk in subtle ways that back-ups on a regular basis are even more essential.

Creating your own web-pages

Creating your own web-pages is not too difficult if all you want is a couple of pages of text. However, designing a series of pages with nice graphics and hot links is a real slog and not to be attempted by the faint-hearted. Of course you need web-space on your Internet provider's server computer to hold your pages once made. This means that even when your own computer is switched off, or disconnected from the web, people from around the world can continue to access your pages. It also means that page access is far faster since they do not have to be sent from your own desk-top modem.

There are many different programs you can use to create web-pages. Several work by allowing you to create whatever document you want as a standard set of pages in your word-processor, which are then converted into the web-page format. The design of web-pages is limited by the constraints of the original specification for how the web works. In order to speed up transmission down the line, all pages are converted into simple elements with few variations. For example, the number or typefaces you can use is limited, unless you cheat by including the text inside a graphic, but graphics can take ages to load.

Hot MetalPro is a web-page maker which is quite powerful – not the cheapest, but it includes many different sample layouts and can handle sound as well as animations and other powerful features.

A common trick is to download a few pages with interesting design onto a hard disk, disconnect from the Net and call up the pages using the web-page maker. The pages should appear exactly as they did the first time. You can then choose an option to see the code used to make the pages (HTML language). It is relatively easy to move things around, change all the text and insert new graphics. The result can be a far more professional effect than if everything was generated yourself.

A good web-page maker will allow you to create a large number of pages, all linked together, and test them as a working system locally before uploading them to your server. Uploading is not too difficult, although once again you may need a friendly voice on the end of the phone to help.

Telling people that you exist

When the pages are finished and uploaded, there is still a further task of advertising. The search engines on the Net will find your pages eventually as they explore the whole network on a regular basis. When they do, a crude index will be formed of key words in the first part of the text, and a reference created for use by all Internet users. In some cases the search engine will permit you to select the key words you want to use, and others allow you to write a brief summary of your page. It's very important to think carefully at this stage, since these key words or summaries will be all that other Internet users see as they decide whether to visit your site or not.

However, the most efficient thing to do is notify the search engines yourself that they need to visit your site. You can do this by calling up the different search programs. They all have a feature to add a new URL, or universal resource locator, the address of your pages. Even doing this you will find that there is a delay of up to two months before the details are processed. Until then you will have to generate traffic another way.

1. Let your friends, family, colleagues, associates, church members know about the site and publish the URL.

2. Contact various relevant newsgroups on the Net and post a message about the site.

3. Search for other groups that have created specialist indexes – say of churches in the same denomination, or of Christian resources – and tell them of your site to add.

4. If you think the site looks very good compared to the usual standard on the Net, and contains innovative features, then try e-mailing a few Internet magazines or the online sections of national newspapers. You may be fortunate enough to be given a review, including a photo of one of your screens.

5. Contact your favourite Christian magazine or newspaper. Ask for the editor and explain that you would like to write an article about starting up a church site on the Net. You may get over a thousand words of free publicity, or at the very least a small paragraph as a news item. Try the other publications too – they are all desperately understaffed and may be eternally grateful for an interesting item to fill the next edition.

Keep your site alive

A good site tends to draw traffic by word of mouth, but to keep people coming back to it you want to offer something of real value to a large number of people that keeps changing. An example might be a superbly researched resource index of your own, which becomes the automatic starting place for tens of thousands of believers worldwide who need a fast way to find out which are the very best Christian sites in particular areas. You could add a sentence or two of your own to each item as a review and give sites your own star ratings for content and presentation. The possibilities are endless.

Another way to generate traffic is to add a piece of

almost irrelevant technology that means the site is automatically listed under other high-profile headings. An example might be installing a video link. All over the world individuals and companies are experimenting with spy cameras, small Internet linked cameras permanently mounted on computers, or linked to them, wired to the Net. These cameras send live images to the Net, usually once or twice every couple of minutes. You can see traffic cameras in various cities, cafés, restaurants, students at work or what people are doing in their homes.

The index of all the camera sites became a high-profile site listed under 'What's Cool' in the Netscape Navigator screen, so huge numbers went looking. Any web-site with such a camera and listed there was likely to receive loads of visits, although of course there is no guarantee that people will stay to look at anything else on the web-pages before searching for another camera.

Going live with cameras and sound

I predict that it will not be long before a number of the larger churches worldwide begin to go live with cameras and sound, allowing people to drop in on live services. Such a step would not be expensive if the link was only operating at certain times. The camera on my own computer can be used to broadcast sound and picture to hundreds or even thousands of others simultaneously for the price of a local call, so it may not be just larger and wealthier churches that want to have a go. No broadcast licences are needed here. How about a remote access training course, for example? The software to view such broadcasts costs nothing, so you can e-mail all your contacts and let them know when to connect.

It would be more expensive to have a permanent line day and night for a camera that basically everyone forgets about. One line could in theory carry images on a rotating basis from several sites – say the church foyer, the main auditorium or church building, the church hall and the church car park. The aim is to convey life and intimacy; to make people feel that they are close to you.

You could even have one in the church office, allowing two-way communication so that those dropping in can alert you to their presence with the option to receive the call, either as a typed message on the screen by someone who can see you, or by voice or even perhaps by a return video link using their own computer linked camera. I am not saying that this is something you will want to do, but we all need to think more creatively.

A scaled response

Many church leaders are already convinced that they need to be on the Net, but they are unsure as to the level. Here is a suggested scale:

1. Small church of fewer than fifty members. Consider e-mail and Internet in the pastor's office for external communications and research. Consider a provider which gives up to half a megabyte of storage free and use it for a personal web-page which is easy to set up with outline details of who you are. Then at least you will one day be indexed and part of the system. Use e-mail where you can to support missionaries overseas. Explore Internet Relay Chat with overseas workers who have Net access. Assess how useful it is to them.

2. Church of 51–150 members. Follow option 1 above and find out how many of the congregation have access to the Net. If more than 25%, consider setting up an e-mail mailing list for important items in addition. Consider a larger web-site or adding your own web-pages to a relevant site owned by another church group or organisation. You will still have your own access points without people having to go through the front pages of your host. It could save time, money and lots of frustration, since there may be a computer expert there who will help you.

Encourage one or two members on the Net to explore ways of using the Net to communicate the good news, perhaps by joining newsgroups or through Internet Relay Chat or e-mail. Experiment with e-mail prayer letters.

3. Church of 151–400 members. Consider 1 and 2 above plus a larger web-site integrating other organisations with whom members have a relationship, and which the church wants to encourage, together with downloadable resources and other extended facilities.

Examples might be a set of indexes leading to seminar/ workshop/teaching resources produced in the past by the church. Consider providing a large list of your own favourite web-sites with a review of each. Consider broadcasting your next day conference on the Net with postings to newsgroups advertising the event. Place a counter on the web-site so you can measure the response.

4. Church of 401–1,000 members. Consider in addition to all the above creating a major innovation on the web, such as a well-advertised link to live worship and links to pre-recorded services, libraries of ministry tapes which can be listened to online or downloaded for future use. Consider a school for training in Internet evangelism, and workshops for other churches as an Internet resource centre. Consider an in-house Internet support service, helping other churches to become Net proficient.

5. Church of 1,001–5,000 plus members. There are further things that a much larger church could consider. Rapid church growth in many parts of the world is resulting in growing numbers of very large churches. The Internet could have a vital role here in countries where a significant proportion of members are online, making for instant communications and almost free distribution of news, rotas, invitations and other information.

Such large churches tend to have very large numbers of

fringe members or past members, now often separated by vast distances. At almost no extra cost, all of these people who so wish can be added to the e-mail lists. In this way, a newsletter containing encouragement and teaching for church members could become an electronic full-scale magazine with a readership of tens of thousands, particularly as receiving it might be open to anyone who hears about it and sends their e-mail number to become an associate member of the church.

Large churches often have a set of smaller associated congregations. For example, Kensington Temple in London now has a combined membership of several thousand people. Of these, some 3,000 meet each week in 100 smaller congregations. Regular e-mail to the 100 church leaders every Sunday morning could mean that up-to-the-minute prayer requests are able to be shared across the whole network. In such a large church it is possible that several hundred might be on the Net, if not more as time goes by. A prayer letter in e-mail could mean that hundreds of believers are mobilised to pray for a particular urgent need as soon as they check their e-mail boxes.

Another thing worth considering is an Internet Relay Chat site for prayer and fellowship. A daring move would be to set this up in a virtual reality world, with church members building a Christian centre of some kind where people can drop by, whether from your church, from other churches, or people who just happen to be passing by. You could advertise it heavily for free. It would be bound to attract a lot of attention. Making it work would require commitment from quite a few people to visit it regularly and help run it.

Interesting sites

The following is a list of sites that may be of interest as part of an exploration of some Christian sites on the Internet. **No responsibility whatsoever is implied or expressed for the content, spiritual or otherwise, of**

sites listed, nor should any listing be taken as an endorsement of the contents of any site or links from it to sites elsewhere.

All of these sites can be located using normal search engines like Excite! or Yahoo or Alta Vista. First try searching under headings like 'Christian' or 'Bible' or 'Church'. You will quickly find yourself linked to tens of thousands of sites.

For the latest demonstrations of new technology and for outstanding new sites, look under the 'What's New' and 'What's Cool' options on the top of the Netscape Navigator screen.

Alphanet: The site of Alpha courses for enquirers to the Christian faith. In 1996 250,000 people were expected to take part.

Hymns: You will find hundreds of hymns in full.

BibleNet: Large resource index.

Christian Cyberspace Companion

Christian Resources Hotlist

Christian Unions in Universities and Colleges in the UK and Ireland

Christian Music Mailing List

Eastern's Bible Dictionary

WWW Bible Gateway

Guide to Christian Literature on the Internet

Book of Common Prayer

Guide to Christian Resources on the Net

Christian Multimedia and Software Centre

Celtic Christianity Homepage

Our Daily Bread

Scripture Studies

Church e-mail directory

Four Spiritual Laws Cell Church

Campus Crusade for Christ

Christian Web Guide

Church Locator

Matthew Henry's Concise Commentary on the Whole Bible
World Wide Study Bible
The Vulgate Bible
The Prayer Closet
Gospel Café Welcome Page
Connected Christianity
Virtual Christianity – Bibles
Christianity Information
New Wine
Virtual Christianity Index
Biblical Christianity
Praise and Worship Music
Biblical Studies Foundation
Religious Art, Icons and Clipart
Christian Children's Games
The Historical Jesus
Crosssearch
Churchonline
Electronic New Testaments Manuscripts Project
Dead Sea Scrolls – Qumran Library

Cyberchurches

Immanuel's Church
First Church of Cyberspace
1st Church of the Internet
CyberChurch
First Internet Christian Church
Prayer Room
Positive Church Cyberchapel
Virtual Church
Web Chapel

Churches with home pages on the Net

There are probably thousands of church home pages. Here is a small sample of some of the most interesting:

Willow Creek Community Church
Champagne Vineyard Christian Fellowship
Yahoo Index of Christian Reformed Churches

Internet Relay Chat

Christian Chat Room
Alphaworld (virtual reality)
Worldschat (virtual reality)

Organisations

March for Jesus
Promise Keepers
Gospel Films
Christian Research Institute
Apologetics (Reason to Believe)

Denominational resources

The Lutheran Magazine
Southern Baptist Convention Churches
The Baptist Page
Anglicans On-line
Baptist Press
Baptist World Alliance
Salvation Army
Pioneer

Newsgroups

Christnet News Groups
  General
  Religion
  Bible
  Christianlife
  Christ News
  Prayer
  Ethics
  Theology
  Evangelical

Philosophy
Ladies
Poetry
Writers
Healing

Soc.Religion Christian
Biblestudy
Youthwork

Glossary of Terms

The world of computers is full of jargon, but much of it is a useful shorthand. Here are some words particularly relevant to the Internet, and some others which will be useful. This is not an exhaustive list.

Anonymous FTP:	Allows public to access FTP site without a password by typing 'anonymous'.
Applets:	Small fragments of programs sent down the line with data and text to run certain activities on a local computer, e.g. animations.
Append:	Add one file to another before transmission.
Alta Vista:	Powerful search engine.
Archie:	Index to thousands of FTP sites.
Archive file:	File containing other files, usually compressed to save time downloading.
ARPANET:	Advanced Research Projects Agency (US military forerunner of Internet).
ASCII:	American Standard for Information Exchange – standard way for computers to share information.
Avatar:	Image selected by Internet user to identify themselves to others using virtual reality systems.
AVI files:	Microsoft movie files.
Backbone:	Network through which smaller networks are connected.
BBS:	Bulletin Board System (qv).
Bandwidth:	Size of the electronic tube through which data is pushed as fast as it will go. Narrow bandwidth means greater congestion. Video and sound uses a greater bandwidth than sending just text.
Binary file:	Any computer file not in ASCII (qv).
Baud rate:	Speed of modem.
Bits per second (BPS):	Number of bits of data transmitted per second.
Bounced message:	Message returned because not addressed correctly.

Browser:	Program used to view web-pages, e.g. *Netscape*.
Bulletin boards:	Computer with a modem dialled direct using another computer and modem, in order to access programs and data on the hard disk of the other computer. No Internet software is required. Access is simple.
Chat:	Users on Internet communicating live, usually by keyboard and screen.
CD-ROM:	CD player on a computer that can play back data and programs as well as sounds/music. Lowest cost method of program distribution apart from the telephone.
Client:	Program or computer served by another program or computer.
Compressed files:	Programs or files compressed to take less space when downloading. They need to be expanded afterwards.
Cyberspace:	Term used to describe the entire world created by those using the Internet.
DARPANET:	Defence Advanced Research Projects Agency Network, forerunner of the Internet formed by combining ARPANET and MILNET.
Dedicated line:	Telephone line exclusively set aside for computer.
Domain name:	Name of a host computer on the Net.
Down-time:	Time computer not available.
Download:	Transfer data from network to your computer.
E-mail:	Electronic mail – can include graphics, sounds, video, files and programs.
Emoticon:	Symbols created in text using a keyboard to express feelings. E.g. :-) is a smiling face. Emoticons used by many people in e-mail messages or Internet Relay Chat.
Ethernet:	Another method of linking computers together.
Explorer:	Microsoft's browser competing with *Netscape*.
Fidonet:	A local network connected to the Internet.
File Transfer Protocol (FTP):	The standard protocol for transferring files between computers using the Internet.
Finger:	Finding information about a user on a host computer.
Flame:	Rude message in a newsgroup or e-mail, can be sent in multiple forms making an e-mail box impossible to use. Often an expression of protest or anger by an individual or group of people.

Forum:	CompuServe term for newsgroups on Compu-Serve system.
Freeware:	Software provided free by the authors.
Gateway:	System allowing two incompatible systems to communicate.
GIF files:	Graphics Interchange Format: images from scanned photographs or other sources. Compressed to speed transmission.
Gopher:	Menu helping people find their way around the Internet, using client and server computers.
Gopherspace:	Anywhere you can reach with a gopher.
Habitat:	VR environment inhabited by many different people.
Hardware:	Metal case, chips, disks, screen, keyboard and every other tangible item that goes to make up a computer system.
Home Page:	First page the user sees on accessing a web-site.
Host:	Computer permanently connected to the Net.
HTML:	Code used in web-page creation.
Http:	Hypertext transfer protocol. The protocol used by all World Wide Web pages.
Hypertext:	A word highlighted on the screen, which when selected leads to other web-pages.
Information highway:	Network of fibre optic and conventional cables running between the main connection points on the Net.
Internet:	Public network of computers.
Intranet:	Private network of computers using layouts and methods similar to those of the Internet. Used by many large companies and banks.
ISDN:	Special telephone line allowing data transfer at speeds up to five times faster than the fastest modem. In practice speeds achieved on the Net may be less due to data congestion elsewhere in the global system.
Java:	Language used to create applets on World Wide Web pages.
JPEG files:	Joint Photographic Experts Group. These files always have the extension .JPG. Used for graphics, especially photographs, especially by newsgroups.
Logging on:	Obtaining permission from a computer system to use its services.
Logging off:	Saying goodbye to the computer connection.

Lurking:	Reading newsgroup messages without adding your own, so remaining unseen and unknown.
Mail reflector:	Mail address which automatically sends any e-mail directly on to a stack of other e-mail addresses.
Megabyte:	Million characters of data (a book can be around half a megabyte long, whereas just one photo can be twice that size).
Modem:	Device used to convert digital signals from a computer to analogue in order to send down copper telephone wires, and to convert signals received back to computer digital data again.
MPEG files:	Motion Picture Experts Group format – extensions .MPG in file names. Video and stereo sound viewed in full screen. Needs a special MPEG board inside the computer, available as standard in many models sold today. MPEG viewer programs can be downloaded.
MS-DOS:	Original operating system of most microcomputers.
Net:	Shorthand for the Internet.
Netscape:	Most common browser in use, and perhaps the best.
Newsgroups:	A kind of bulletin board where people can exchange views, files, graphics and other information with others round the world. There are more than 5,000 such groups, increasing rapidly, of which 200 are devoted to adult topics.
Newsreader:	Program allowing you to read newsgroup messages and contribute.
New server:	Computer on which newsgroup is based.
Online:	Computer connected to computer network.
Packet:	Small amount of data, part of a longer transmission.
PC:	Personal computer – usually means IBM compatible.
Plug-ins:	Small downloadable programs which give browsers added features, e.g. sound and video.
Point of presence:	Connecting to a service locally, even if the main computer system is a long way away.
Posting:	Message sent to newsgroup.
Postmaster:	Person responsible for overseeing the running of a mail system.
Pretty Good Privacy (PGP):	Encryption software used to make sure that no

one can read a message except the person for whom it is intended.

Public domain software: Software not owned by anyone which can be used freely.

Server: Large computer used to store web-pages for global access.

Service providers: Companies providing access to the Net.

Shareware: Software freely distributed for which payment is expected if the program is found to be useful.

Signature: Message generated automatically to go at the end of an e-mail communication or newsgroup contribution.

Software: Programs that control what computer does.

Surfing: Following one link to another to another, jumping from site to site using computers all over the world, all accessed from one PC on the Net.

Switching: Sending packets of data via different routes to make maximum use of all capacity available on network.

SIT files: Compressed files for Macintosh computers.

TCP/IP: Transmission Control Protocol/Internet Protocol – rules on how data is transferred on the Internet.

Telnet: Direct dial of computer systems, often with their own log-in requirements, rather than access via the World Wide Web.

Token Ring: Small local network which may be connected to the Internet.

UNIX: Operating system used by many larger computers, including most Internet hosts.

Upload: Sending data or files from your own computer to another on a network.

USENET: 'User's Network' – large network connected to the Internet.

UUE files: UUencoded files, compressed for use by newsgroups.

Virtual reality (VR): Computer system simulating a three-dimensional world. With special green and red spectacles a three-dimensional image can be generated on an ordinary computer screen. Alternatively, VR may be just two-dimensional images which change in a way that allows three-dimensional exploration. An example might be where the user can explore a spaceship, turn corners, go down escalators, and whatever direction the person takes looks just like a video of a person travelling along that particular route. These simulations are becoming important in industry, medicine and architectural design.

Virus:
Computer program that duplicates itself and spreads from computer to computer without the intended action of the users. May trigger unpredictable damage to systems.

VT100:
Standard terminal configuration used by Digital Electronics Corporation and adopted widely.

Web-page:
Page of text and/or graphics created on the Internet using HTML language.

Windows:
Graphical interface created by Microsoft to replace MS-DOS. Latest version is *Windows 95*, which comes with Internet software fully loaded as a standard feature.

WINSOCK:
Program to make the Internet work with *Windows*. Different versions may be needed for different browsers in order for them to work correctly.

World Wide Web (WWW):
Hundreds of thousands of pages all linked together.

Zip files:
Files compressed by a standard PKZIP program.